FINDING
BITTERSWEET

KEN PIERPONT

ISBN: 9781092772105

DEDICATION

This book is dedicated to my friend
Charles Perlos

And to those of you who prayed for us and supported us
during The Red Jeep Journeys.

With reverent and grateful thanks to our sovereign God,
who brings sweetness from bitter things.

TABLE OF CONTENTS

PART ONE: THE RED JEEP JOURNEY

PART TWO: BITTERSWEET FARM JOURNAL

PART THREE: THE CHARLES PERLOS STORY

FINDING BITTERSWEET

Imagine you are sitting in the back of the chapel at a youth camp in northern Michigan. In the front of the chapel are two stone fireplaces. It's a cool, early summer night. Small fires are burning to take the chill off the night air. You might hear me say something like this to the campers:

> *"For those who love God,*
> *when something bad happens to you —*
> *God is doing something good."*

God was about to teach me that lesson in a deep way. It would be a bittersweet story, one I would never tire of telling.

PART ONE:

THE RED JEEP JOURNEY

CHAPTER ONE

COLD SPRING

Springtime was coming to Michigan. After a long, snowy, icy, frigid winter, you long for evenings with a glass of iced tea out on the porch, the blossoming of the flowering pear tree out front, the appearing of the daffodils, the warming of the earth, and the music of birdsong in the morning cool...

But for our family it was a cold, dark spring. Our family was in turmoil. The arrival of spring brought no joy to any of us that year. We were deaf to the song of the birds, blind to the color of flowers, too brokenhearted to bask in the warming of the earth. Life for us was too hard, too cold, too confusing to notice.

Like so many things in life, what happened was at once good and bad. It was both sweet and bitter. I'm convinced that God was in it and I'm sure Satan was behind it. As painful as it was, I never want to forget what happened that year. Never. That is why I'm telling this bittersweet story now.

I gave ten of the best years of my pastoral life to a church in the suburbs of Detroit. In the tenth year, a small, self-appointed group turned on us to push us out. It was a time

of great injustice. I resigned without a job or anywhere to
go.

The Red Jeep Journey
We prayed for direction and sensed the leading of God to
begin an itinerant ministry while we sought God's direction
for the future. I had a seventeen-year-old red Jeep. The
body was clean, but it had more than 250,000 miles on it.
We would trust God to enable the Jeep to get me wherever
I was invited to speak.

Two questions loomed: Would I have enough places to
speak? Would I be able to gather enough money to meet our
basic needs? Family members were depending on our help
and support. How would we ever be able to help them with
no job, no income?

For years I had considered the possibility of becoming a
full-time speaker, but the circumstances never seemed right.
Now, uninvited, the adventure of being a full-time speaker
lay directly ahead. It was terrifying, it was sad, and it was
exciting all at once. It was not my choice, but I became a
full-time itinerant speaker.

I changed the oil in the Jeep. I bought new tires. I washed
and waxed and prepped my little Jeep for the road. I
prayed for supporters. I called camp directors and pastor
friends and offered my services. Immediately the preaching
calendar began to fill with opportunities large and small.

The Fellowship of the Red Jeep
I contacted friends and appealed for financial support.
People who supported us with prayer or a one-time gift or a
monthly gift were affectionately dubbed "The Fellowship of

the Red Jeep." There were twenty-two families in The Fellowship of the Red Jeep; we will not forget them. Each member of The Fellowship of the Red Jeep has a unique story; some of them I will tell.

The Red Jeep Journal
I determined to keep a journal along the way. I would create a travel narrative of the adventure, it would make good reading, and I would use it to tell our interested friends about what God was doing. I had a powerful confidence that God would go with me; I would not be alone. I knew there would be wonderful stories to tell. They would be more precious to me than I could have imagined that spring.

Red River George
For you to understand The Fellowship of the Red Jeep, The Red Jeep Journey, and The Red Jeep Journal, I must first tell you the story of the red Jeep. Anything we own of value has a story attached to it, and this was true of my red Jeep. Years ago my wife, Lois, received an inheritance. She set her heart on buying a VW New Beetle and asked me to help her shop for one. As we looked through ads, I was distracted by a beautiful Jeep Cherokee Classic with alloy rims and tinted glass. It was red on red, a glistening little truck. I loved it. For years I had considered this my dream car but never thought of actually owning one myself. I was sure Lois would love it. She is a photographer, and I knew it would serve her well in her photography business. I talked her into a test drive, and immediately she said, "Let's get it."

She waited in the car while I negotiated a great cash price. It would be perfect for her. After we drove off the lot, she stopped and said: "Let's swap cars. You drive the Jeep, and I'll drive your car. The Jeep is for you."

"What?" I said, moved with emotion.

Lois isn't comfortable with too much emotion. "Let's not get all sentimental about it," she said, not looking at me. "I'm just embarrassed by the car you drive."

And just like that, I owned a red Jeep. She would go on to buy her own car, but she used her own money to buy me my dream car first.

Lois's people are from the mountains of Eastern Kentucky, and they worked hard for years to earn the money that bought that car. They were from a region near the Red River George, a beautiful place in the Daniel Boone National Forest. Her grandfather's name was George. He died before I met the family, but I knew his wife, Lois's "Mamaw," Ruth Hatton, and I named the Jeep after George —hence the name "Red River George" or "George," sometimes called "The Red Jeep." He would be the iconic symbol of my itinerant adventure that would begin, ironically, with a trip into the mountains of Eastern Kentucky to preach. God knows how to write a good story. Never doubt it.

So, the travel journal would be "The Red Jeep Journal," and my adventure was called "The Red Jeep Journey."

CHAPTER TWO

GOING FORWARD WITH A BROKEN HEART

After I resigned from the church, I started my Red Jeep Journal with these words:

What's Next for the Pierpont Family

We served a church in the Detroit area from 2007 to 2017, accomplished much, and made some wonderful, lifelong friends. Now it is time for a new chapter in our lives. We will be prayerfully seeking our next place of ministry. It's an exciting adventure. We are now in full-time itinerant preaching, storytelling, evangelism, and writing while seeking another flock to shepherd. (I think Lois has a few projects for me too.)

The Red Jeep Journal

Here is the good news for you...I will be creating a travel journal as I travel and speak. On Monday, April 11, I leave for the mountains of Eastern Kentucky, where I have been asked to conduct spiritual enrichment meetings at the Oneida Baptist Institute. It will be springtime in the mountains. (My Kentucky girl may travel with me on this one.)

George (my red Jeep) and I will travel to youth camps, family camps, retreats, churches, schools, colleges, banquets, couples' events, men's events, etc.

This week our youngest daughter, Hope, and I labored hard to box up my entire library—thousands of books. I will be working from my Jeep and from my cozy study at home. Looks like my trips will take me from Northern Michigan to the Upper Peninsula to the mountains of Kentucky—even to Canada. Of course, I plan to travel to Oregon and Texas to visit family, and I will be open to ministry opportunities around there. We will gratefully go through the doors God opens for us.

Gospel Conversations and Evangelism
As I travel to speak and between assignments, I will be encouraging and counseling believers along the way and doing what I can to make Christ known to everyone I meet. I am planning to have gospel conversations on the journey. It is my goal every day to "nudge" everyone I meet a little closer to Jesus.

In my next entry I will tell the story of a wonderful conversation I had recently with a couple of ladies I met at a bed-and-breakfast...

Granville Cottage
March 18, 2017

I knew it was important to stay upbeat in The Red Jeep Journal, but deep in our hearts there was great hurt and sadness. I'm not a worrier, but I found it hard to sleep and hard to eat, wondering what the future would hold. During this sad and confusing season of our lives, we sat in our family room and wondered aloud for hours about what God was doing. We knew him well enough to trust him, but still we wrestled with feelings of anger and fear. We lay awake in our bed at night and tried to turn our hurt and worries into prayers.

It was a time of uncertainty and deep pain. I tried to connect with friends in ministry and let them know of our availability, but I was almost 60 years old, and many churches and ministries do not want to invest in someone so close to retirement age. We considered a number of churches and had a long conversation with a Christian camp looking for a director. We tried to stay open to anything the Lord might be doing with us.

CHAPTER THREE

THIN PLACES

One weekend Lois and I were invited to meet with the pulpit committee of a church in need of a pastor. This story, which I included as part of The Red Jeep Journal, comes from that experience:

> Recently we stayed in a bed-and-breakfast in a small Midwestern village. Sun's up; it's morning; I'm at one end of the breakfast table. Two ladies are at the other end. We are sipping coffee and orange juice. Lois is skipping the breakfast for the same reason I am there — because there are strangers in the room.
>
> The ladies are managing a charity that involves a historic estate. I ask them to describe it. Both agree there is something very special about the estate, and they tell me that people love to visit the place during times of national or personal turmoil.
>
> "It's a peaceful place. It's as if it is haunted by good angels," they say.
>
> For a while they go on to describe some of the experiences they have had and some of the people

11

attached to the place, including the eccentric woman who lived there all her life. She left the estate to the foundation, along with an endowment to provide for the cost of maintenance.

I ask if they have heard of "thin places."

"They say there are places on earth where the distance between heaven and earth, the spiritual and the material, is thin," I explain.

They nod in agreement.

"This would be a thin place," they confirm.

This launched a lively exchange: they eagerly ask questions and tell stories, and I answer the questions and tell a few stories of my own.

A fruit dish is served. We pour more coffee.

I tell them that I am a Christian writer and speaker, and I explain to them how to understand the spirit-world according to the Bible. They listen, cups in midair. Time moves quickly in the lively exchange about ultimate and eternal things.

Suddenly they realize what time it is. They are going to be late for their symposium.

"Oh, we've got to go. It was so good to meet you, so interesting to talk," they say.

After a satisfying give-and-take, they ask for my business card. I give them my name.

"Google it. I'm all over the 'net. I've written over a thousand pieces that are archived on my site. You can read the stories, watch the videos, and listen to the podcasts."

That is what it looks like. My travels took me to a small Midwestern town where two ladies who were fascinated by spiritual things now have a little clearer understanding of the world according to the truth of God.

When I returned to the room, Lois was packed and ready to go. We checked out and found a little bakery downtown where we could enjoy some coffee and fresh-baked pastries and where Lois could enjoy her breakfast from a social distance that was a bit more comfortable.

But for a while, the place was thin. We live *Coram Deo*— in the presence of God. All places are thin; we just aren't always aware of it. In lively conversation with strangers over breakfast, we can sometimes thin the distance between heaven and earth.

Granville Cottage
March 25, 2017

There is a little more to the story that I didn't tell in the Journal. The town we visited was small, and the bed-and-breakfast was modest. It was stately and historic, but it was very modest. As soon as we had arrived, I could see that the nice man who ran the place was trying hard to make a go of things and wearing more than one hat.

When he showed us to our room, he mentioned that our bath was down the hall. When he left, we noticed the door didn't have a lock. Lois said: "Can you pull the dresser in front of the door? I don't feel safe."

I tend to use the men's room during the night, so I was conflicted, imagining the urge to get down the hall quickly in the dark at 3 o'clock in the morning and the necessity of trying to wrestle the big dresser away from the door first.

As I lay in the bed that night, sadness came over me. Finally I feel asleep, but in the middle of the night I lay awake in an unfamiliar bed, thinking over what was happening and wondering what the future would look like. I thought of the little dark-eyed girl whom I had met in Bible college. My heart went back over the years of ministry, our partnership, her loyalty, the goodness of God. I didn't want to wake her, but I wanted to touch her. I reached out in the darkness and put my hand on her arm. Finally sleep came.

In the morning as we were dressing, she said, "Why did you put your hand on my arm in the night?"

"Because I love you," I said. "I love you so much. You've been such a loyal and faithful companion to me all these years, no matter what we've been through. I love you."

It was a beautiful sunny day. We drove to the church and had a delightful interview with the good people there, but it was clear to us both when we got in the car to head home that it was not the place for us.

CHAPTER FOUR

A BITTER DISAPPOINTMENT

When I resigned from the church, the deacons promised me ten months' severance pay and hospitalization insurance. I took comfort in knowing that I would have some time to raise support or find another place of ministry. During that time I talked to all the full-time itinerant preachers I knew, and they were very encouraging. To a man, they were candid and said that I would have to learn to live on very little.

One afternoon I called Tommy Oaks. Tommy walks with the Lord. He is a full-time traveling preacher from Tennessee and one of the best storytellers I have ever heard. I'll tell you a little more about Tommy later. My conversation with him is one I will never forget and always cherish.

I asked Tommy about raising money. He opened his heart and told me about his own sweet and simple journey of faith. He did not try to enlist monthly supporters; he simply lived on what the Lord provided. He lived simply. He drove an older car. His home was very modest. He had all he needed. God used him. God provided for him.

During the conversation I mentioned the promised severance pay. He was quiet on the other end of the line, and when he spoke he said, in his slow, Tennessee drawl: "Well, Ken, I don't really know about that severance thing. In my experience, a man almost has to prostitute himself to get that severance."

"Here is the way I see it," he said. "If you are going to become a traveling preacher, you are going to have to learn to depend on the Lord to meet your needs. If you are going to learn to depend on the Lord to meet your needs, you might as well start right now."

Immediately, I knew those words were from the Lord—for me. In a few days I would find out why. Soon I would discover that there would be no severance pay. Instead of being paid through the end of the year, my pay stopped immediately. We had no income. We had no health insurance. We were going to learn to depend on the Lord, and we were going to begin immediately.

We were shocked and we were afraid. The disagreement with my brothers at the church was deeply painful. As hurtful and frightening as our circumstances were, I sensed a great freedom from the Lord. I had clearly been released from my sense of duty to the people I had pastored for ten years, and I was free to concentrate on my writing and speaking. I was dependent directly on the Lord for our daily bread. I felt rejected by the church, so like the apostles in the Book of Acts, I shook the dust off my feet and went to the next town to preach the Word.

I experienced a mixture of sadness, betrayal, adventure, and freedom. I had no income. People were actively attacking my reputation, but I was fully dependent on the Lord. I consoled myself with the knowledge that God knew my heart was pure and I was a full-time traveling preacher.

Sometimes truth comes to you as clearly as if Jesus had walked into the room and spoken to you eye-to-eye. When Tommy said, "If you are going to be an itinerant preacher, you are going to have to learn to depend on the Lord, and if you are going to learn to depend on the Lord, you might as well start now," it was one of those moments for me.

The months ahead would deepen our trust in the faithfulness of God and his care and love for our family. We would find that God had placed his people all over the country, and each one would listen to our story and help us along the way on our new adventure as a "keeper of the story."

CHAPTER FIVE

KEEPER OF THE STORY

I've been preaching since I was 14, pastoring since I was 17. In decades of preaching and teaching, I have grown in my conviction that careful teaching of the Scriptures, passionate preaching, and storytelling are powerful allies in delivering truth. I believe all preachers and teachers of truth should be concrete and clear in their communication. They should answer these questions:

—Can you make that clear?
—What does that look like?
—Why do I care?
—How can I do that?

I have learned, from the way God has gifted me, that telling stories is a powerful way to communicate clearly. Not all good preachers and teachers are good storytellers, but I believe that those who don't choose to use stories should be clear and concrete in their teaching. I also believe that those who choose not to use stories should avoid blanket statements that condemn or denigrate those who do.

How I came to love stories is one of the best stories I ever tell. I tell that story in an earlier book: *For a Few Days*. (You

18

can read it there.) The story of how I came to love stories has many chapters; it's a book I hope to be writing for years to come. I want to add a chapter now before I go on telling the story of The Red Jeep Journey.

A Spring Night in the Ohio Countryside

Years ago in central Ohio, a friend invited me to attend special meetings at a country church. We drove to the little stone church through hilly farm country in fragrant spring. I didn't expect much, but I was in for a pleasant surprise. My imagination was ignited that night by a storyteller. His name was Tommy Oaks.

Tommy is from Tennessee. I understand he was the first man ever to graduate from East Tennessee State University with a master's degree in storytelling. I love the sound of that, though, degree or not—I'm sure Tommy would say you can either tell a story or you can't. You don't have to have a master's degree to be a good storyteller.

When I went to hear Tommy, he was wearing a plain shirt with a string tie. He had a salt-and-pepper beard and had a little more hair on his face than on his head. He moved the pulpit aside and spoke without notes. He had in his memory what he was going to say, and he skillfully planted his messages in our hearts. This is what he said: "When I was a boy, I went to church a lot. The preacher always had three points and a story. I couldn't tell you what the points were later that afternoon, but I always remembered the story. Tonight I want you to remember what I am going to say, so I am going to tell three stories and make one point."

He told a story. It was a good story, and when he finished the story he didn't make any point but simply said: "Alright,

that's the first story. Now for the second one," and launched
into another. The first story was short and humorous. The
second story was simple and short too. Then Tommy said,
"That's the second story; now here's the third."

The third story was slower in the telling, and it was serious.
Everyone, even the little ones, held still and breathed quietly
and followed Tommy with their eyes. By the time he
reached the end, you could start to discern the truth that
tied all three of the stories together, a profound and weighty
truth. It didn't seem like Tommy had talked for a long time,
but looking out through the open window, you could see
that the sun had slipped from sight and the fireflies were
hovering over the grass. The air was cooler, and all of us
sitting on the wooden pews enjoyed the silence that a good
story produces. We listened slow, like we were smelling
fresh bread or sipping good coffee.

Both And: Theological Faithfulness and Storytelling Skill
In the circles in which I run (that's right—I run in circles),
we are pretty theologically conscious. We take a dim view of
messages that are not rooted in Scripture top to bottom. We
have a carefully drafted doctrinal position, and we like to be
able to tell that our preachers are sticking pretty close to it.
We don't really think the pulpit is the best place to express
our personal opinions or preferences. We like some meat in
our preaching. We want to hear someone handle the Word
of God with skill and passion.

When liberal theologians abandoned the authority of
Scripture around the turn of the nineteenth century, they
exchanged them for moralistic stories about social themes.
As a result, we often rightly assume that storyteller
preachers don't quite have all their theological marbles.

They aren't always playing with a full theological deck. They are armed but they are no danger to the enemy because their homiletical gun is loaded with blanks.

Tall Tales or True Truth

I met a guy like that a few summers ago. He was a very good storyteller. I was eager to hear him because he was a pastor. He was from a denomination that is not well known for wearing out their Bibles, so I was not surprised to find that he was not obsessed with truth. His specialty was tall tales. He sure could spin out a yarn and lay a whopper on you — sort of a liar for hire, I guess. You could tell from listening that his was a sort of smorgasbord theology: you take what looks good to you, and if you see something that you don't think would taste good to you, you just leave it alone.

After he "told," I talked to him. I congratulated him on his skill and his style. I said, "I understand you are a pastor."

He must have seen what was coming or read my mind. Before I could speak again, he offered: "Don't try to make any sense of my stories. They are strictly for entertainment."

I smiled politely, but the idea went against my grain. I don't think I have ever told a story without a specific lesson or point. As I see it, if you don't have anything to say, that tells me something. You are making the point that you don't think it is important to make a point. I'm not suggesting you have to assault people with truth. If you tell a good story, you shouldn't have to harangue them to get a point across. A good story well told mostly applies itself. You just lay it on the table and walk away.

My favorite preachers are storytellers who know the Story of stories and tell it well. The stories of the Bible are often left untold or they are not told well. Secular storytellers commonly tell tall tales, myths, and legends. There is a place for different kinds of stories, but my own niche is true stories. Usually I know they are true because they happened to me, but in my storytelling repertoire, I also have a few well-chosen favorites that I have picked up from others.

In my view, it is illegitimate to tell stories in the pulpit and try to make a point with them if you don't believe there is a major "overarching story" that gives purpose to all the other stories. They say that post-moderns are wary of an overarching, unifying narrative. That's too bad, because there is a meta-narrative, a "big story" that ties the little stories together. God is the author of the great Story, and it gives meaning to all other stories ever written. To reject the big Story is to lose your place in the Story of God.

Jesus, the Master Storyteller
Jesus fulfilled the prophecy of Psalm 78 by being a storyteller. You can tell a lot about Jesus by the commands he gave, the questions he asked, the prayers he prayed, and the stories he told.

Do you remember when Jesus told three stories to make one point in Luke 15? You have to agree that in telling three stories he made one of the most memorable points any teacher ever made. The first two stories climax into one of the most powerful stories anyone has ever told—the story of the Prodigal Son. Jesus told three stories about lost things found. In every story, everyone rejoiced when the lost things were found, including the father. At the end of the third story, there was a twist—an exception: there was one who would *not* rejoice.

The older brother, he refused to rejoice. The father comes out into the night and pleads with him to come in to the the party, but the story ends before we know if he does. People will be telling those Jesus stories long after he returns. They are powerful.

My Ambition

Men are filled with ambition from boyhood. They want to fight fires, fly to the moon, populate planets, win championships, subdue kingdoms, and capture fame, honor, and beauty. I just want to be a really good storyteller. My ambition is the Kingdom of God, and my calling is to stir people up to press into the Kingdom with the Story and with stories.

I was off on a mission to tell the Story that has changed all our lives and the stories of people who believe and some who won't. I was a keeper of the Story—in a red Jeep.

CHAPTER SIX

SPRINGTIME IN THE MOUNTAINS

Early in April we sent out a Red Jeep Journal entry to our friends.

The Word Does What No Man Can Do

George is getting ready to go on the road—George is the name of my red Jeep, but that is a story for another day. He got an oil change, and we checked his fluids and aired his tires. I even spent some time in prayer over him, asking God to extend his life and bless the miles over which he will carry me to bless people. While I pray these days, two things in particular preoccupy my mind: Where will I speak, and who will be on the team?

Where Will I Speak?

I will drive to the mountains of Eastern Kentucky next week to begin. I'll tell you all about it in The Red Jeep Journal. God has allowed me to set up meetings in both peninsulas of Michigan, Ohio, Indiana, Tennessee, Kentucky, and Ontario, Canada! My calendar is filling up with preaching engagements. I will be busy—very busy. For that I am thankful to the Lord.

Then there is the other question...

Will You Join the Team?

We are working now to quickly line up a team of people who believe in what we are doing and want to be part of it. Some have already joined. I cannot tell you how grateful to God we are for them…and for folks who are believing in what we are doing, praying, showing interest, and sharing a monthly gift of some amount.

The Word Does What No Man Can Do

A few years ago, Lois and I were asked to speak at a couples' banquet. It was a really simple affair but a sweet time. We had dinner and I spoke. I opened my heart honestly and did my best as always, and I didn't feel it was particularly polished or outstanding. A few months later, I found out that God used that talk to bring marriage revival to a husband and wife who were there that night. I didn't know. That is the way God works. He uses his Word to do what only he can do.

To share a monthly gift, send me an email (and I will explain how to do that), or use the Donate button on my website. Thanks so much for helping. I will keep sending The Red Jeep Journal entries so you all can enjoy being part of what is happening. Thanks for praying for us as we start this new journey.

Granville Cottage
April 2, 2017

Our First Official Trip

The day before leaving for my first official trip on The Red Jeep Journey, I visited a friend at Open Door Bible Church in southern Michigan. Driving out in my red Jeep that morning, I noticed that the greening of the year was approaching. It was warm; the grass was growing again. I enjoyed a warm, encouraging time of fellowship with my friend that day. God had placed him in my path; that was clear.

That Sunday afternoon I visited a young man whom I had led to the Lord and baptized a few years earlier. He and his girlfriend and her mother wanted to help me along the way. That day, they prayed with me and wept and gave me gifts. His name was Shawn. Shawn walked me out to my Jeep, reached in his pocket, and then handed me fifty dollars. We prayed and I thanked him deeply from my heart and drove around the corner and filled the gas tank of my Jeep with that money.

I stood there on the warm April day just praying that God would provide many more tanks of gas for George. I committed the ministry to the Lord in prayer and drove to the next place. We were not at all prepared to experience what God had for us in the next six months.

I am not given to worry, but we were dealing with great pain, betrayal, and painful slander, and our hearts were heavy with unanswered questions. To be honest, those thoughts did keep me awake at night some. Lying in my bed, I wondered why God would allow such an injustice to happen to our family.

The Mission Begins
On Monday morning, April 11, 2017, the mission began. I packed my things, put my sleeping bag in the back of George, and prayed with the family before heading south.

It was a sunny spring day as I drove out of Michigan and into Ohio. My little Jeep faithfully purred down the road. I was alone with the Lord. I kept crying out to him in prayer as I drove. I kept thanking him for all the years of ministry he had allowed me to have. As the miles passed, I thought about how, over the years, God had given me my heart's desire to be a pastor and to preach his Word every week and to tend a flock and encourage people in the Lord.

God owed me nothing. A sense of that powerful truth swept over me. If this was the end of my ministry, I would never charge him with unfaithfulness. He had been so good to us. He had given me the desire of my heart for almost forty years. If the injustice to my family and the slander of others brought my ministry to an end, I would still serve him with all my heart for the rest of my life.

Ever since I was 17 years old, I had been paid a regular salary as a pastor, except for the few years I was in school. Now, for the first time, I did not have a dime of salary. I did not have hospitalization insurance. We needed to help other family members who were facing huge expenses. We had a lease payment that we would have to pay—for the rest of the year—for Lois's photography shop. Our youngest daughter, Hope, was planning to leave for Bible college in Oregon. There were many expenses, but there was no income.

As I drove through southern Michigan and Ohio that spring morning, the radio was silent. I had a powerful sense of the presence of the Lord with me and I kept turning my worries and thoughts into prayers.

During those months I often thought: "Lord, you have allowed me to be paid to preach the gospel all these years. You owe me nothing. If you are going to call me to faithfully proclaim your truth at my own expense, I will. If you call me to be the greeter at Walmart, I will do it with joy. But Lord, you will have to strengthen me."

Unsure if I would have enough money to buy lunches on the road, I planned to pack a lunch and enjoy the hospitality of my hosts along the way. A little after noon on that warm April day, I drove through Cincinnati and crossed the Ohio River into Kentucky. At the top of a long hill, I pulled into a rest area and took my little lunch cooler to a picnic table in the sun.

When I bowed to pray that afternoon, inexplicable joy flooded my soul. It really made no sense. I was in real trouble. I had no income. I had no insurance. We were being slandered and wondered if anyone would want us to speak or pastor again. Our family was passing through the deepest waters. The stinging injustice of it all was suffocating, but in the middle of all of that I discovered that when I got into the Jeep and turned the key and the little engine sprang into service, over and over again God flooded my heart and soul with joy.

I had a cold bottle of Ale 8 in my lunch that day. Down in the mountains of Kentucky, just a few miles from where Lois was born, they bottle a sweet ginger ale they call Ale 8. On family trips to Kentucky when the kids were small, we would always stop and buy Ale 8 for everyone as soon as we reached Lexington. It was a cherished family tradition. In my heart's eye I can see them all now: small children in the van, each holding a green glass bottle. I choked back tears at the memory of it.

I ate my sandwich and apple and washed them down with the soft drink, and something sweet happened in my spirit as I sat there at that picnic table in the sun. God comforted my soul with a deep comfort. It is impossible to explain, but it sustained me. It would happen over and over again, but for now I had promises to keep. It was time to head south.

CHAPTER SEVEN

IN THE SEASON OF DOGWOODS
AND REDBUDS

My next entry in The Red Jeep Journal was from my first preaching assignment.

Oneida Baptist Institute

This week, I drove into the mountains of Eastern Kentucky to speak at Oneida Baptist Institute during their annual Spiritual Emphasis Week. From Natural Bridge to Oneida, the road follows the South Fork Kentucky River. The dogwoods were opening in the woods, and the redbuds were showing off their purple blossoms all along the winding way. I walked to and from meals and speaking times across a swinging bridge over Goose Creek. It was a wonderful way to welcome spring into my soul.

My dear friend Sam Judd led the worship. Sam is a delightful young man with a deep love for the Lord, a genuine heart for people, and an advanced understanding of the Scriptures. The young men and women listened and responded well. Each night, students came at the conclusion of the messages to pray at the altar. I preached messages on what to do when life doesn't make sense, what to do when life hurts, what to do when you feel unloved, and what to do when you are crushed by guilt.

Oneida is a boarding school with students from around the world. On the final night, a young lady from Tanzania gave her life to Christ. After chapel that night, Dr. David Price, Sam Judd, and I prayed and said our goodbyes.

As Sam and I stood and talked into the night, a full moon rose over the mountains in the east. The conversation with Sam alone would have made the trip worthwhile, but there also would be many additional deeply satisfying conversations with people who not only were devoted to the Lord but also consciously dependent on him. It was good to meet them and hear their testimonies of the faithfulness of God.

I will return to the area to speak at the Kentucky Mountain Mission in June for teen camp and return to Oneida to speak at a pastors' conference in July.

The new ministry as an itinerant preacher has begun. On Easter Sunday I will preach in Bremen, Indiana, and on Sunday, April 23, I will preach in the morning service at Gilead Baptist Church in Taylor, Michigan.

Granville Cottage
April 13, 2017

The Things You Hear

On the road, I was the keeper of the Story. I was a gospel preacher. Over and over again I told the story of how Christ came to live the life we could never live and die for us so we would not have to die. Along the way I listened to the stories of others.

In the spring of 2017 I was especially eager to hear stories of God's unusual providence in the lives of those he loves. At the Oneida Baptist Institute, the chaplain is a man named David Price. I asked David a question that I asked wherever I went on The Red Jeep Journey.

"David, have you ever had an unusual experience of God's guidance, or providence, a time when you felt God spoke to you in your heart?"

When you ask that question of people, it often triggers a time of fascinating conversation. He said; "Yes, I have."

"When my father died, I went home to take care of things and I was looking through some papers in the attic. I came across some financial papers and realized for the first time that when I went off to college, my father took out a second mortgage on the house to pay for it. I graduated from college and made my way in life. My dad worked into old age and died without ever telling me what he had done to see to it I could have a college education."

He added: "Another story involved my son who graduated from Bible college and took a place of ministry out in California. I agreed to rent a truck and help drive him out there with his things." They drove out to California together, enjoying the time together, knowing they would be living a long way away from each other.

"Dad," his son said, "have you ever smoked a cigar?"

"No, son. I don't smoke," David said.

"I know, Dad, I just thought it might be neat to smoke a cigar on the way out since no one else is around. It would just be us."

David agreed and shared a big cigar with his son. By the time he got to where he was going that night, he was a very sick man. In the middle of the night, he made his way to the drug store for some relief.

There was a young woman working alone in the store that night, and she seemed troubled. My friend David talked to her and comforted her by asking her if he could share a passage of Scripture with her.

"Sure," she said.

He quoted a passage of Scripture and she immediately began to weep.

"Earlier tonight I was so discouraged," she said through tears. "I was thinking of my grandmother. She went to church. I loved her. I know she loved me. But she died. She used to quote a Bible verse to me all the time. Tonight I was trying to remember that verse and I couldn't remember it. Then you came in, and that is the verse you just quoted."
On The Red Jeep Journey, I would tell stories everywhere I went. Between "tellings" I would listen to other people tell

stories by the fireside, along the lakeshore, overlooking mountain lakes, over food, walking in the forest. Telling stories, listening to others tell their stories—there is power in it.

At Oneida, one of the buildings had a wide porch filled with a dozen white, wooden rocking chairs. Before walking over the swinging bridge to my quarters, I would listen and tell stories to whoever would join me until I was all alone, and then I would call Lois or one of the children and we would encourage one another. Those were sweet conversations there on the porch at night, with the sound of crickets and the cool mountain air.

It was an adventure. It was something I had often thought about. I wondered if it was something that God would have me do full-time. Now I had no choice. Suddenly and without warning, I was a full-time itinerant preacher. It would be a test of our faith.

CHAPTER EIGHT

A TEST OF OUR FAITH

Shortly after we started The Red Jeep Journey, a pastor friend whose church was just up the road from the one I had served befriended me. He invited me to speak at his church on the Sunday after Easter.

During this time I had called all the camps and pastors I had spoken for in the past. One of them was a pastor in Atlanta, Georgia, who had had me speak a couple times before. He was remarkably generous both times. After I promised my pastor friend up the road that I would speak for him, the pastor from Atlanta called and asked me if I was available to fly to Atlanta and speak.

I was tempted to ask my friend to release me from my promise, because I needed funds and the pastor in Atlanta would give me a very large honorarium. I heard my dad's voice in my head: "Kenny, do what you said you would do. Always keep your promises. God blesses that."

It was clear what I needed to do. I would keep my promises, and I would go where I first promised to go—no matter what other opportunities came. I would take the opportunities as they came, and I would trust the Lord to take care of us. That would be my policy.

That Sunday I preached for my friend. He was very kind, and his church and his people were very generous with us and encouraging. They received the Word with great openness and sent us on our way that sunny spring day.

We thanked our pastor friend for his kindness and support, and we thanked the Lord for giving us our daily bread. Later, when my pastor friend found out what I had done, he laughed and said: "Ken, you should have gone to Atlanta. Their gift would have been six times what ours was." But God would supply without our having to resort to manipulation and without breaking our promises.

After church that day, Tom and Diane Hansbro took us to the Round House for good fellowship and BBQ. Tom and Diane were loyal friends. During this time I sat in their home and told them my plans. They were in deep pain for us, and they determined they would be our patrons on The Red Jeep Journey. They supported us with overwhelming generosity every single month.

When I would drive way from a camp or conference, I would always call my parents or the kids and tell them about the triumphs of the gospel from the week, and then I would usually call Tom and Diane and they would rejoice with me. They were always so encouraging. To have someone believe so deeply in us at that time of testing was a powerful thing. Tom would always watch my messages online or read my stories and invariably comment with two words: "Good stuff."

Another Test of Our Faith
In the next Journal entry I will mention preaching at Bremen, Indiana. On the Saturday before Easter I said

goodbye to the family and drove away. I would drive to my parents' home in Hillsdale County to shorten the trip on Easter.

The fellowship with my parents was sweet in their little country parsonage. They were suffering with us and at the same time encouraging us to cling to the Lord during this trial. They were assuring us that he was faithful. I lay in the upstairs bedroom of their little country home listening to the sounds of the countryside and trying to calm my heart and prepare my soul to be a blessing to the people in Bremen on Easter Sunday.

I had promised to preach for the Easter sunrise service and the regular Easter service, so it was in the dark, early morning when I pulled away from the parsonage in George.

I celebrated Easter with the good people of Bremen. Our niece Emma and her boyfriend (now husband) Morgan came to hear me. Other than that, no one said much of anything to me. I walked out to the Jeep, hung my blazer on the peg in the back seat, and headed for back to Michigan. Being apart from my family on Easter Sunday was hard; I missed being with them.

When I left, no one gave me an honorarium check. I didn't expect the honorariums to be enough to live on, but I did hope the gifts would at least offset my travel expenses. It was an oversight that the church quickly corrected, but on that Easter Sunday afternoon, my heart was heavy as I drove way.

How was I going to possibly make it financially? How would I meet my obligations, pay my bills, buy gas and insurance, and pay the upkeep on the car? How could we help our family members who so desperately needed our financial help at that time?

As I drove along, my phone rang. "Hello?"

"Uncle Slim. How are you?"

It was my nephew David. On an Easter Sunday afternoon, he was thinking of me. My heart was tender toward him. He had suddenly lost his father about two and a half years earlier. We talked about his dad. Just as his dad would have done, David asked me a lot of questions about our speaking ministry, and before we hung up, my spirits were lifted when he promised to send monthly support for our ministry.

All during The Red Jeep Journey, generous gifts would show up in our account regularly from David. Every week or so my phone would ring, and David would sincerely inquire about the progress of our ministry. It always reminded me of his dad, who was always so sincere in his interest and generous in his support.

Whenever my spirits were low, God would lift them. On Easter Sunday evening, I arrived home safely to gather with the family in the family room and tell the first stories of The Red Jeep Journey. There would be many remarkable stories.

The First 300 Dollars
In March of 2017 I got a call from the daughter of Helen Barth, who asked me to give the eulogy at her mother's funeral. This was an amazing honor for me.

Helen Barth was a very popular Christian singer when my mother was a young Christian; Mom listened to the music of Helen Barth continually when I was a boy. Mom considered her an informal voice teacher and mentor in ministry. The church in Dowagiac, Michigan, where my mother's family began to walk with the Lord, was founded by Helen Barth and her husband, Reinhold.

Helen Barth had a music ministry with Moody Radio that spread all around the world during that time. She was a radiant and anointed musical minister of the gospel.

During this season I was thinking about how often churches seemed to be looking for younger men. I was speaking at camps to children and teens, and I was among the oldest wherever I went. It makes you think. Thinking of Helen Barth and other faithful, older saints I wrote this:

When Wrinkles Discourage You
Jesus said our words reveal the content of our hearts. I was teaching a small class one day when one of the ladies opened her heart in an unusual way and revealed a dark thought that lay in the bottom of her soul. It was troubling.

She said: "When my husband left me, I had a lot of life still ahead of me, and I thought I was a catch for someone, but now years have gone by and no one seems to want me. Now I feel like I am going to grow old and die on the couch—old and wrinkled and alone."

The room grew silent with the pain of her admission. Immediately I recognized that what she had just shared with me was a lie that the enemy had embedded deep in her soul. Jesus would never tell his daughter something like that...he would never say to his beloved daughter, "You are going to die alone on the couch, old and wrinkled." He has brighter plans for his daughters than that.

Helen Barth was my mother's role model as a pastor's wife and as a singer. This spring I gave the eulogy at her funeral. Helen was lovely in her youth and radiant in her old age, despite the wrinkles that lined her face. Even in old age, her voice was beautiful and her testimony was powerful. The years of faithfulness to God only added to the impact of her songs and her stories.

Have you ever seen a picture of George Beverly Shea or Ruth Graham? Their faces were wrinkled, but they lived meaningful lives and died surrounded by people who loved and admired them not because of their physical strength or beauty but because of their spiritual vitality.

Corrie Ten Boom was plain in personal appearance, and it was hard for her to move around when she was released from the Nazi prison camp, but she called herself a "Tramp for the Lord" and traveled all over the world telling the story that there is no pit so deep that God is not deeper still. She was wrinkled, but she was not lonely.

Amy Carmichael served the Dohnavur Fellowship in India for fifty-four years with hard, unrelenting labor. It was spiritual warfare. I'm sure it took its toll on her. Before they laid Amy's body beneath the birdbath that marked her simple grave, no doubt her face showed some age, but those who knew her said she glowed with an unearthly radiance.

I watched Elisabeth Elliot hold the attention of thousands of people as she spoke of God's faithfulness to sustain her through the loss of two husbands. She was poised and well-dressed, but her influence was not dependent on her appearance.

Wrinkles don't have to take away from your radiance, because radiance does not depend on youth. Radiance comes from deep within—from a spirit alive with God. It shows up in your life and in your face, and it is more powerful than the wrinkles and baldness and bulges and aches and pains that slow us with age. Praise be unto our Eternal God!

Don't let wrinkles discourage you. If God is your Father, you have life that is eternal. One day you will step from this life into eternal life in the presence of God! Your outward person may be wasting way, but your inner person—your spirit, is getting stronger every day! Live like you believe it, with a smile in your heart and a spring in your step!

Preaching at Helen Barth's funeral was a great honor, but I realized it was a special grace from the Lord for my mother. I picked up Mom and Dad on the way to the funeral in northern Indiana. It was a wonderful service that included Bert Kettigner from Moody Bible Institute and Al Smith's son Johnathan.

At the end of the service, they gave me a generous honorarium of $300. I knew immediately I would give it to my mother. When we said goodbye that day, over her strong objections I gave that money to my mother as a gift to use in any way she wanted.

At that time I did not know it, but within a few weeks we would begin the ministry of The Red Jeep Journey and we would be seeking support for the work. The first gift that came into my account for the ministry was in the amount of $300. Mother gave the honorarium I had given her from Helen Barth's funeral back to me so that I could preach Christ to young people that summer.

CHAPTER NINE

THE MOST WONDERFUL PLACES ON EARTH

My next Red Jeep Journal entry was written on a special day.

Hope America Is an Adult

Our baby turned 18 today, so we enjoyed our annual birthday brunch together. Hope America is probably headed to the Oregon coast in the fall to attend a Bible institute.

This Sunday at Gilead in Taylor

This Sunday morning at 10:30, I will preach in the morning worship service at Gilead Baptist in Taylor. Last week I drove to Bremen, Indiana, and spoke three times on Easter Sunday morning. It was a beautiful drive that also allowed me to visit with my folks the night before. This summer I will be in a camp or conference every week except the week of July 4th. Imagine preaching every morning and every evening almost every day this summer. Speaking of camp, here is a story from camp that will help you see how powerful the camp experience can be.

One of the Most Wonderful Places on Earth

A few summers ago at camp, a teenaged boy camper came up to me to talk after chapel. He was an eager camper. He was verbal and engaged. His family situation was very difficult because his mom had died that year and his dad had troubles of his own, beyond being a single dad.

"What church do you attend?" I asked.

"I don't really go to church, but I used to go to AWANA, and the people from the church paid my way to camp."

Our daughter Hope was a camper that week. One evening she was sick, and I took her to town for medicine. It was late at night when we drove back toward camp through the night. The car was quiet. The car lights shown out onto the dark road ahead.

"Dad."

"What, Hope?"

"You know that boy who came up to talk to you after chapel?"

"Yes?"

"He caught me out in the woods during ambush tonight..."

"Really?"

"We walked in together. He said something I thought you should know…"

"What did he say, Hope?" I asked.

"We were just walking in and he said: 'Isn't this the most wonderful place in the world? Everyone loves you here, and they all talk about Jesus. I just love this place.'"

Later in the week I sat with the boy, and we dangled our feet in the lake and talked. I encouraged him to return to volunteer as a worker and attend High School Week the next summer.

The week after camp, his dad called me and told me that he had picked him up from camp and driven him to Indianapolis. Dad said, "He talked nonstop about camp all the way to Indianapolis."

When I returned to camp the next summer, the staff told me that the boy already had spent two weeks there that summer. Maybe someday he will be the camp speaker — it really is one of the most wonderful places on earth. Everyone loves you there, and they all talk about Jesus all the time.

Granville Cottage
April 20, 2017

Vance Havner
I have an orange, well-worn, little hardcover book in my library. It is a treasure to me. People often ask me when they see how many books I own, "Have you read them all?"

"Some of them I have read over and over," I sometimes say.

This little orange book is one of those. Something about the stories in the little orange book captured my soul. The title is *Three-Score and Ten*, and the author is Vance Havner, who was a traveling preacher.

I discovered his books in the Adirondack Mountains of New York one summer. His little book titled *Pleasant Paths* would have an impact on my life. Reading *Pleasant Paths* helped me discover what kind of preacher I wanted to be, the kind of pastor I wanted to be, the kind of Christian I wanted to be, and the kind of writer I wanted to be.

Most of the books on Christian ministry that I read at the time did not seem to make a place for rest and reflection. There was continual pressure to perform and little ink given to the cultivation of the inner life. Even the Lord Jesus often went away to the mountains or spent time alone in the wilderness between seasons of intense ministry among people.

Reading Havner reminded me that there was a sacred rhythm of work and rest, quietness and service, in the life of Jesus. There in the mountains of Upstate New York that summer, sitting in an Adirondack chair overlooking a lake and reading *Pleasant Paths*, I determined that I would find a place of ministry where I could establish such a sacred rhythm in my own life and ministry. I also determined that I would buy and read every book Havner wrote. I did both. Reading Havner, I realized that most of his books were fifty short chapters long.

I'm a bit hyperactive, but I was more so in my youth. It occurred to me one day that I could write a book a year by writing a simple, short chapter every week, a practice I have continued to this day. As a result, I have faithfully maintained a blog with a post at least once a week for the last twenty years.

Vance Havner's book titled *Three Score and Ten* was written as collection of his memories from his traveling and preaching. For years I have picked up the book and read the stories of God's direction and protection and provision, and they always thrilled my heart. Now I would be traveling in the red Jeep and writing stories of my own.

I love to read travel narrative, especially narrative that follows the advancement of the gospel and chronicles the stories of people who gave themselves to Christian mission. My Red Jeep Journal entries would be travel narrative, my own stories of God's work in and through my life. Part of it thrilled me—even in the midst of the painful injustice our family was facing.

In April and in May that year, I was preaching every weekend. Beginning in June, I would be gone all week for the entire summer, preaching at camps and conferences during the week and at churches on the Lord's Day.

When there was a gap in my calendar, the Lord filled it. Every single week. Every single weekend that I was available, God sent me somewhere to preach.

One evening during this time, I took a phone call from a trusted ministry associate in whom I had invested much. The conversation took a cold turn when I realized that he had turned against me. It was a very sad phone call. I said nothing to him, but when I quietly hung up the phone my heart was broken.

I explained to my family what had happened. As we sat there in quietness, I could tell that my family was hurting for me. Just then the phone, still in my hand, rang. On the other end of the line was a camp director from the Finger Lakes Region of New York. He had a camp week that had opened, and he needed a speaker. I had only one open week left. They were the same week.

Everyone in the room that evening could tell what had happened. The Lord had arranged the timing of the call to encourage me when a trusted ministry associate turned away from me. This kind of thing would happen all through the spring and summer. Some people had turned their backs on me, but God would not. He said, "I will never leave you or forsake you," and he promised his disciples on the mountain in Galilee that as they went to make disciples, he would be with them always, even to the end of the age.

As I got in the red Jeep to go make disciples, God was present with me. The sense of fellowship, the feeling of well-being, and the peace and confidence that I was doing what I should be doing never left me, no matter where I went. I was never alone in my red Jeep that summer.

My next Red Jeep Journey entry would take me to the state of Ohio.

Keeper of the Story

God's truth is life-transforming and powerful. I love to teach the story of God and apply it and illustrate it with memorable stories. Because of that, sometimes I call myself a "keeper of the Story." A few weeks ago, our son Chuk passed this little nugget of a story along to me. Let me pass it along to you.

Flying and Fishing

The pilot always looked down intently on a certain valley in the Appalachians when the plane passed overhead. One day his co-pilot asked, "What's so interesting about that spot?"

The pilot replied: "See that stream? Well, when I was a kid I used to sit down there on a log and fish. Every time an airplane flew over, I would look up and wish I were flying...Now I look down and wish I were fishing."

See what I mean about stories? A story is a gift you can give away to others and treasure it still yourself.

Adventures with George the Red Jeep

On Sunday, April 23, I was invited to be the guest speaker at Gilead Baptist in Taylor, where Tom Downs is pastor. It was a delightful morning. The worship was meaningful, and the people were very receptive. It was good to connect with new friends and old. Our friends and supporters Tom and Diane Hansbro came to hear us that day. After church they treated us to some great BBQ, so it was a good day.

This week I spent some time building our support team. I drove to St. Clair to meet some new friends (and figured out that St. Clair and St. Clair Shores are not the same city). We are grateful to the growing group of friends who believe in what we are doing and are helping and encouraging us.

Next week, "George" will take me to Ohio so I can preach at Bailey Road Baptist Church, and then I will spend a few days with my brother Nathan and brother-in-law Jim at a pastors' conference in Chagrin Falls, Ohio, near Cleveland.

Stay in touch. Let us know if there is any way we can help you.

Granville Cottage
April 28, 2017

CHAPTER TEN

INEXPLICABLE JOY

A Thoughtful Kindness

There is a sweet story about the people of the Bailey Road Baptist Church in Ohio that I have never told before. When they originally contacted me, they were in search of a pastor. I was open to whatever the Lord had for us at the time. I had a good conversation with the chairman of the pulpit committee, and he scheduled me to preach two weekends in a row. As the time approached, more and more I realized that I did not want to make myself available to a church so far from our daughter and her children, who would need our support. I called and told them that I would be eager to speak but that I would not be able to candidate to be their pastor.

A couple weeks later, the chairman of the pulpit committee called back and asked if he could schedule a potential candidate to speak on one of the weeks they had originally given to me. I willingly agreed. Then he said something that showed great thoughtfulness: "I know you are scheduled to attend the pastors' conference in Cleveland, so we want you to come that week and we are going to get you a hotel room that night so you can attend the conference without any additional travel or expense."

I drove to Bailey Road Baptist Church and spoke, and after the evening service they took me out for dinner, and we enjoyed an evening of fellowship and conversation before we parted. I got a good night's rest and was refreshed for my conference the next day.

At that time of rejection and sad disappointment, it was sweet to know that there were people of God out there who were thoughtful and loving, who would go to special expense to demonstrate love and thoughtfulness to us. Along the way of the red Jeep, that would happen over and over again in ways that gave me strong confidence that God was with me and that God was for me.

Here is my entry from The Red Jeep Journal that week.

> Last week I preached at Bailey Road Baptist and then attended a conference at Parkside Church in Cleveland, where Alistair Begg is the pastor. It was a great time of fellowship, singing, preaching, laughter, and good food. My little brother Nathan and brother-in-law Jim Evans were with me.

> **George the Red Jeep**
> George the Red Jeep is a very important part of our new traveling ministry. He is seventeen years old, but he runs well, looks good, and gets me where I need to go. I feel a special joy when I check his fluids, pray, turn the key, and start off down the road to wherever God has assigned me. Today I will replace his windshield glass, the better to see the beauty of God's creation on the way to speak to God's people.

Last Sunday I preached at the Open Door Bible Church in Hudson, Michigan. It is in beautiful Hillsdale County. Saturday I will preach at a men's retreat in Rose City, sponsored by Oakwood Community Church, which is pastored by my friend Don Jackson. I will travel to South Litchfield Baptist Church on the Lord's Day (Mom and Dad's church). Next Sunday I will head north to St. Clair, Michigan, to speak at Crossroads Community Church.

Thanks to The Fellowship of the Red Jeep
Jesus's ministry was sustained by the gifts and hospitality of people who believed in him. He went about teaching and doing good. In a similar way, the Pierpont family has been sustained financially by the gifts of God's people who believed in what we were doing. It's still that way. Thanks so much for all of you who have been a part of our team.

Granville Cottage
May 16, 2017

While there was a sense of adventure in The Red Jeep Journey, a dark cloud of sadness and injustice always followed us. Our daughter had been treated with cruelty and injustice. One evening while I was out on the porch, I noticed a plant in the corner and recorded these thoughts:

He Makes All Things Beautiful in His Time
One of the saddest days of my life was the day our daughter Heidi came back home. She fled an abusive husband with her children and the few things she could hurriedly pack into her car, while her husband cursed at her and threw her things out the door, down the steps, and onto the lawn.

I quietly helped her unload her car and carry her possessions into the house. One of the things I carried into the house was a plant. It was ruined. I wondered why she hadn't found a place to throw it away. It was ugly and broken.

"Do you want me to throw this away, Heidi?" I asked.

"No. I want to keep it."

I set it on the porch. It was a bit of an eyesore, but she wanted it. When I thought about it, I watered it. She wanted to keep it, so I watered it. It was broken and it was not beautiful, but I made up my mind quietly, without saying anything to anyone...that plant was going to live.

One day I was on the porch reading, and Lois came out and watered the plant. She said: "This plant is going to live. Heidi wanted to keep it. I made up my mind. It is going to live."

Over time, with tender care, it did live, and more than live, it began to flourish into a thing of beauty. A few months later, Heidi sold it for $40. Since then, God has helped Heidi to flourish too. He has given her a joyful spirit. He has provided for her needs. He has sent good people into her life who care for her and cherish her.

Saturday morning I drove up north into the peninsula that is Michigan to speak to a group of men about what it means to be a man. I showed them from Genesis that man was created to take dominion over the earth and bring it into the beautiful order of God's dominion. I showed them that Adam and Eve were given a dominion on earth and they were to make life flourish in that jurisdiction. They were to bear children and subdue the earth and till and keep the soil and make things grow and bring order and beauty to God's world.

I told the men about the ugly, broken plant and the story about how with time and care it became a thing of beauty. The room grew quiet, and the men leaned into the story. With his life a man can create a safe and orderly place where people and things can flourish and grow. He can deepen the curse, or he can bring the blessing and favor of God to the people in his life.

Jesus said to pray for those who abuse you, and that is what I do. I pray that those who abuse will one day find repentance and be restored to fellowship with God and make right the wrongs they have done. I have found a place of mercy at the foot of the cross. I would never deny a place to any repentant man.

An Encouraging Opportunity

When word got out that I was available, I got a call from Jeremy, the pastor of a large church that had a campus near our neighborhood. I had admired the ministry of this church over the last ten years, noticing their energetic and successful outreach, especially to young people and young families. Pastor Jeremy needed a campus pastor for the Riverview Campus. We got along well and had some rich conversations. He invited me to consider the opportunity. I was greatly honored, especially at that time in my life. I was feeling a little "put out to pasture" because of my age.

Jeremy said: "Man, you have two strikes against you. You are old and you are Baptist. We would have to train you in our system, but everybody I talk to around here who knows you is excited about bringing you on."

I smiled. It was a great encouragement to me at the time to be considered at a fine church, especially one that was sound in theology and progressive in their ministry approach—especially for an "old Baptist" like me. I didn't go to Metro City Church, but I will always consider it an honor and an encouragement that they were willing to talk with me about it.

Lois and the family would often attend Metro during the summer while I was away. It was refreshing for them during that season in their lives. Heidi especially loved the fact that the church was focused on ministry to young people. She needed all the encouragement she could get with what she was facing.

In June, my summer schedule began. I would be on the road all summer speaking daily at camps and on the Lord's Day at churches. I would be gone from home, and I would not be able to see the family or Lois, but I knew what I had to do. I had to stay on the road. I was eager to serve the Lord and make him known. It was an adventure, and I never wanted to lose the romance of it.

Lois agreed and never complained. From the early months of our marriage, I had realized that Lois was a strong and loyal companion in hardship. Our whole family was powerfully united against the hardship and injustice that we were facing.

There would be people to meet. There was the ministry of the pulpit that would open the heart of people to face-to-face ministry. I loved both kinds of ministry. I would be spending my summer in pulpits all over the Midwest and talking to people over meals and over campfires and walking in the mountains on the lakeshores.

It reminded me of a preaching trip I had made to the Canadian Rockies a few years before. I included this story in an edition of The Red Jeep Journal:

Johnson Canyon

I like to tell the story of my visit to Johnson Canyon in the Canadian Rockies. The water roaring down through the rocky riverbanks of the canyon was a unique hue of blue-green. I asked our host and guide Jared, "Why is the water that color?"

He said: "It glacial water. The water is from snow melt high on the mountains. From early fall into late spring, snow gathers up in the mountains. When it melts, it runs down through this canyon, carrying minerals that give it that blue-green color."

People who know me know that I am a storyteller. But I don't tell stories to entertain. I tell the stories of the Bible, or I tell stories to illustrate or apply Bible truths. Getting the truth of the Bible into your soul is like snow on the mountains. Sometimes learning Bible truth has an immediate effect. More often it is like snow on the mountain. Over the weeks and months and years, it melts and runs down into our lives and makes life flourish.

I get to teach the Word all summer long and into the fall in churches and in camps. According to the promises of

God, it will bring life to those who receive it. (Read Isaiah 55:9–10.)

On Sunday morning after preaching in St. Clair, two people came up to me and tearfully said: "Pastor, that message was for ME today...It was for ME..." It is a powerful thing to simply read, explain, and apply the Word of God to the lives of people. After over four decades of ministry of the Word, it still surprises and delights me to have someone tell me about that powerful effect of the Word of God. That is what I get to do almost every single day all summer long in about five or six states and two countries.

Thanks for praying, and thanks for those of you who are sharing gifts to keep George the Red Jeep on the road so I can teach the Word like snow on the mountains.

Oakwood, Crossroads, Bremen
Since I last wrote a Red Jeep Journal entry, I spoke to a men's group called Band of Brothers, sponsored by Oakwood Community Church and pastored by Don Jackson; drove into beautiful Hillsdale County to preach at Mom and Dad's church; and last Sunday, I discovered that St. Clair Shores and St. Clair are different cities with similar names. I had a delightful time preaching in both services of Crossroads Community Church in China Township, Michigan. On Sunday I will return to Bremen, Indiana, for morning and evening services.

Granville Cottage
June 1, 2017

A Band of Brothers

"Though you have not seen him, you love him. Though you do not now see him, you believe in him and rejoice with joy that is inexpressible and filled with glory" (1 Peter 1:8, ESV).

The morning I left to preach to the men from Oakwood Community—they called the group "Band of Brothers"—I had the experience of joy in a very powerful way that would overtake me time and again on The Journey of the Red Jeep. It was as if I would turn the key and joy would flood into my heart.

My task was simple and straightforward: go and preach the Word. Listen to people. Pray with people. Encourage people. Enjoy meals with people. Go about doing good. I was made for this. I was called to this. I was thrust into this, at least for a time. There was a great sense of well-being and joy in it, even though it was a painful time for all of our family. God was near; he is near to those who have a broken heart. He was faithful to pour out the fruit of the Spirit. I could powerfully sense his presence in that little red Jeep. Prayer and praise came easily as I pointed that little Jeep toward my next preaching assignment.

The organizers of men's retreats are careful to plan food that appeals to men. It makes me smile when I think of it. When I preached to the Band of Brothers, I would need to leave as soon as I was finished to get where I needed to be on the Lord's Day. As I concluded my speaking, I could smell the steaks on the grill. It's the last thing I would experience as I drove away: the smiles of the men and the smell of steaks on the grill.

I had to leave before the steaks were ready, but I would not go hungry on The Red Jeep Journey—not at all. God's people would take good care of me._

The Bethel Church

Just a few weeks after walking away from my former church, I received an email from the Bethel Church in Jackson, Michigan. A friend, Bill Rudd, had recommended me to a church through a friend, Jim Lacy, who was the interim pastor. The people of Bethel were looking for a pastor. I arranged to drive over to meet with their pulpit committee, but I could not imagine ever really opening my heart again to a group of people. I never wanted to take my family though such an abusive ordeal again.

It was a sunny, spring Wednesday evening when first I drove into the parking lot of the Bethel Church in Jackson. We talked for a few hours with the committee. In spite of my hurt, I opened my heart and told them the whole sad story of what had happened to our family. I wondered if I would ever hear from them again.

The Summer Begins

Early in June I started off in the red Jeep for a conference in Tennessee and my first week of camp at the Kentucky Mountain Mission in Eastern Kentucky. My little grandchildren Keira and Koen helped me wash the red Jeep. I packed my things, prayed with the family, and headed south.

The Summer of the Red Jeep had begun. I drove away quietly that morning, wondering what lay ahead; it was clear that our calendar would be full. Would our financial needs be met? The youth camps cannot pay enough to live on. We would need to have help from friends who believed in what we were doing. We knew that unless we had the special blessing of the Lord, our venture would fail.

The previous October we had signed a year's lease for a building for Lois's photography business. Now our lives were disrupted and there would be no significant income from the building, only continual expenses, including a monthly lease payment of $800. We would have travel expenses. Hope was planning to leave for Bible College in the fall, and she would need a car. There would be expenses for tuition and travel. Heidi and her little ones would need our financial support, and she would need thousands of dollars to defend her parental rights—and she had no income. We were cut off without hospitalization insurance.

Our daughter Hannah was married to Dale, who grew up in the church I pastored. He was a deacon, and his heart was broken over what had happened. Hannah and Dale would come over to the house and sit with us in the family room and we would try to make sense of what had happened to us. Dale and his brother resigned from the deaconate in protest over the way we were treated.

In all of this I had a sense of peace. We turned our worries into prayers when we were burdened in the night. We called out to God when the children were sad and unsettled. We prayed for God to keep our hearts tender and trusting in the face of such injustice and betrayal, and the little cabin of the red Jeep was a place of sweet fellowship with God as I drove from one preaching assignment to the next.

CHAPTER ELEVEN

A Stone for a Pillow

Here is the first Red Jeep Journal entry as summer began:

Tennessee and Kentucky

Last night I stayed in Lois's sister's home on the way to Tennessee. Her children, Faith and Bobby, were excited to see me, especially since I arrived with hot pizza and cold Pepsi. Bobby eagerly helped me in with my luggage.

They asked what I wanted to watch on TV. I told them that if they would turn off the TV, I would tell them stories. For the next couple of hours, we swapped stories. For the last hour I answered their questions about the Bible. The last question 11-year-old Bobby asked was "How can you know you will go to heaven when you die?" I pillowed my head with a deep satisfaction, amazed at the insightful questions such young children had about the Bible and hopeful that a rich faith would take root in their little souls.

Riding the Local

Vance Havner was an itinerant preacher in a different era than I was. He never drove a car and rarely flew in a plane. Most of all he liked to get to his preaching destinations by train, and when he got there he loved to walk. In his little book titled *Pleasant Paths* he wrote of "riding the local." In his day, there were express trains and local trains. The express train stopped only at major cities. The local trains made stops in all the little villages and towns along the way. Vance liked riding the local. That way he met more passengers taking short rides and he took in the local character in each little town and village along the way.

The other night I was making my way across south-central Michigan. I could go south and take the Ohio Turnpike, a quick but boring affair, or I could take the well-traveled, familiar, and efficient Interstate 94. Instead I followed my nose south across country, knowing that I would have to eventually cross Old U.S. Route 12 — The Chicago Road...the route that connected Chicago and Detroit in the day before the interstate highway system existed. I took Route 12; it was like "riding the local."

For my efforts, I was rewarded with undulating roads through the countryside that passed trim farms and rural homes. I enjoyed the view of a sky-blue lake in the evening light. I could smell the BBQ from a roadside stand and paused for a farmer making his way in from his fields on his faithful old International Harvester. As evening set in, I cruised slowly down the main street of a delightful Michigan town I had never visited before, enjoying views of stately, well-preserved homes set back from Main Street, shaded by mature maples back into full leaf from a long winter.

With a few exceptions, I won't have to rush this summer. I have a very full schedule, but I will have time to pace myself. Once George the Red Jeep gets to the camp or conference grounds, he will have a week to rest until he carries me to my next preaching assignment. This summer, for the most part, my plan is to "ride the local" and take in the sights when I can, eat at the local diners more often, frequent roadside stands, talk with people—just see where God sends me and whom he wants me to encourage.

Meeting a Fatherless Boy
The other evening on such a journey I stopped in a coffee shop, and God had arranged a meeting with a fine young man named Ben. His dad was a pastor who had attended the same collage as my dad but had died suddenly a few years ago in his fifties. Ben and I talked at length, and before I left we were both convinced that God had arranged the meeting to encourage Ben.

As I aimed my Jeep west into the declining sun, I wondered if Ben's dad had asked the Lord to send someone to his son that evening to encourage him. This would not have happened if I had not prayed before I left, sitting out in front of the house, asking God to direct my path and make me a blessing. That is the kind of thing that happens sometimes when you "ride the local."

Middle Tennessee
June 9, 2017

In some of the most unusual and beautiful places, God has opened doors for me with people who love the Lord and whose hearts have been touched by my writing or my preaching. Sometimes the doors opened to me have given me opportunities in coveted places of ministry, but usually the places God has allowed me to go have been simple and modest. Sometimes I stayed in spare bedrooms in private homes.

There are those who hear me preach. There are those who read what I write. They are my people, my ministry. They tell others. Simple invitations come. When I can, I go. During the summer of The Red Jeep Journey, I did not have a church, and I was open to take almost any invitation. I took all of them that I could. Early on in the journey, an invitation came from Tennessee.

The Mahoneys

Friday through Sunday I was a guest of the Mahoney family in Tennessee. They hosted me in their home and treated me with great kindness. The night I arrived, we had dinner around a huge table. They have ten children (that is not a typo). I arrived just in time for salmon and broccoli around a huge wooden table beside a huge fireplace. After dinner they took me to town to a cute little place where we had frozen yogurt before they showed off their town. We closed the evening with a song. One of the daughters played the piano, another played a flute, and Dad played the guitar. We had Bible reading and family prayer before bed. (Okay, I may have told a few stories.)

On Saturday we did a family seminar at their church. It was a delightful time. In the afternoon they drove me into the mountains and we hiked out to a beautiful place called Stone Door. The view was worship-inducing. On the way home they stopped by a wonderful local BBQ place, and we literally feasted on pulled pork and smoked wings. (How did they know BBQ is my love language?)

I complained that there was not enough singing on Friday night, so on Saturday night Dad (Thomas) led the whole crew in a couple of hours of singing hymns and songs that became kind of "Jewish-sounding" somewhere toward the end of the second hour and turned into joyful dancing. I watched Thomas and his children interact. Anyone could see the deep love the children had for their dad and their mother, Donna.

On the Lord's Day morning, Dad was up with some of the others making a wonderful breakfast. If I've ever had better pancakes, I don't remember it. We smeared them with real butter and drowned them with real maple syrup. The family had me inscribe their copies of my books and then surprised me with a beautiful hardcover copy of Leland Ryken's biography of J. I. Packer. (I made a mental note to post my book wish list online more often.)

Liberty Cumberland Presbyterian
That day I preached in their delightful church, the Liberty Cumberland Presbyterian Church. It is a beautiful red brick colonial and is filled with hospitable Southern people. Their worship was beautifully liturgical. I am not used to that, but it was sweet to experience it. There was a time of confession early in worship.

I loved "The Passing of the Peace." I had a sense of the presence of the Holy Spirit looking a brother or sister in the eye and warmly blessing them with "The peace of Christ be upon you."

They allowed me time for a full message and received it warmly. As I sat on the platform waiting to preach, a Tennessee memory came back to me that I don't remember ever telling before. I told the story to open my message.

"When I was about 14 we were on a family vacation and saving money by camping out and eating from the cooler at roadside rest stops and parks. We came into a little Tennessee village one morning and stopped near the town square and began to lay out our breakfast on the trunk of the old Chrysler, as I recall. An old gentleman saw us, noticed our out-of-state plates, and opened the town hall to us and made us welcome.

"I will be on my way out of town in an hour, and we may never see each other again. Would you extend a warm Tennessee welcome to me?"

I asked the Tennessee people of the Liberty Church to open their hearts to me and welcome the message of the Word. They did. After tears, prayers, and pictures, the Mahoneys drove me to the edge of town and waved me off.

A Token of God's Favor
I aimed the red Jeep back toward Kentucky. A few miles from town, I pulled over to the side of the road. The pastor had given me a check. A woman had pressed

some bills into my hand. I slipped them into my pocket. I pulled over to see how much I had been given. We were just beginning. I knew we would have enough places to preach. Would we be able to pay the bills?

When I glanced at the gifts I had been given, my heart became humble and full. The little church had given me $800. The camp would give me $450 that week. A friend sent $400 that week. My heart was filled with thankful praise. This was my first week. We received gifts totaling $1,650. Our bills would be paid.

I drove along the beautiful highway thanking God that he was blessing The Red Jeep Journey and The Fellowship of the Red Jeep. We are well-fed and healthy. Our bills are paid. I had gas in the red Jeep.

In an hour and a half I drove across the border from Tennessee into Kentucky and followed a narrow, well-paved, winding road that connected two major highways up over a mountain. At the peak of the mountain, a deer was standing calmly by the side of the road. I stopped in the road a few feet away, rolled down my window, and took her photo. It was as if she posed for me. I drove way. She never moved.

No one will ever convince me that God has not poured out his grace on The Red Jeep Journey so far. Thank you to all who are a part of The Fellowship of the Red Jeep. My heart is filled with great joy to use my little Jeep to make Christ known. I pulled into tidy grounds of the Kentucky Mountain Mission in time to preach again before a good night's rest.

Kentucky Mountain Mission
June 10, 2017

The Mahoney family was a faithful monthly supporter of The Red Jeep Journey, and they still listen to our messages and read our stories. I will always cherish the memory of my visit with their family.

In the mountains of Eastern Kentucky, just a few miles from the Daniel Boone National Forest, is a ministry called the Kentucky Mountain Mission. The mission owns a summer camp, and I was asked to speak to the teens that summer. I built in plenty of time to travel there without the kind of haste that deadens the soul. The roads were clear and lightly traveled that Sunday afternoon. I took the back road that followed the ridges of the mountains into the camp that early summer afternoon, arriving at camp in time to get settled into the tidy speaker's quarters, hang up my clothes, arrange my things, check my email, and take a little hike. It was teen week. Campers would arrive in the morning. My next Red Jeep Journal entry included this story about one of the campers:

William King
The first night of camp up in the mountains of Eastern Kentucky, I noticed William. William was a tall boy with red hair, not the kind of red hair that chooses you, but the kind of red hair you choose. It was not auburn or rust; it was red, really red. It was cut high and tight and stood up straight on top, and it was red as a fire engine. He was getting a little distracted during my talk the first night. I made a mental note to try to keep things moving and hold his attention.

Most kids will listen if you work at it a little. Some are determined to ignore you, and every once in a while you will find one who seems like the devil himself may have planted him just to distract others. I wondered what William's story was and what category to put him in. I should know by now not to be too quick to plug people into categories. William's story would start to come out soon.

After lunch, the next day I found a group of boys hanging out in a group. William was among them. You couldn't miss him. He was taller than everyone, and he had that shock of red hair on the top of his head. We made small talk for a bit, about basketball and breaking your ankles, and then William said, "I only have one ankle."

Kids are full of jokes, but I had a hunch he was serious. I said, "William, are you serious?" He pulled up his pant leg to reveal a prosthetic leg, ankle, and foot. The other boys grew quiet.

When he was 4, William was riding with a family member on a lawn mower. He slipped off the back of the mower and his leg went under the deck. They rushed him to the hospital, but they could not save his foot and ankle and part of his leg. Because William had lost so much blood, the doctor told them they should thank God that he was alive.

We all sat overlooking a quiet lake and line after line of blue and purple mountains out into the distance, and we talked about why God would allow such a sad thing to happen to a little boy.

Thank God for places where kids can go to process the pain that they experience in this beautiful but broken world we live in, places with Bible answers and people who listen, good food, fun things to do, and time for eternal things and ultimate questions.

Fruitful Ministry
John Piper said, "The true usefulness of our [ministry] will not be known to us until each fruit on all the branches on all the trees that have sprung up from all the seeds we've planted has fully ripened in the sunshine of eternity."

Only the Lord knows the eternal fruit from our ministry, but many campers made decisions for salvation and decisions to consecrate themselves to God. Some of the campers this year reminded me that they had been saved when I spoke there last year. Many professed faith in Christ this year. I wish you could have seen the mountains or heard the campers sing. I wish you could have seen them after chapel, lifting their hands up to the Lord as a sign of their consecration to God. I wish you could have been there around the fire on Thursday night. You would have wept as you listened to their sweet testimonies of God's work in their life.

Kentucky Mountain Mission
June 17, 2017

CHAPTER TWELVE

MEETING GOD OUT ON THE POINT

While I was speaking at the Kentucky Mountain Mission, every day I would start the day by hiking out to "The Point" at sunrise. The Point was an escarpment on the camp, high over a valley that looked out over mountain after blue mountain. In the mornings a mist rested in the mountains, and the air was full of birdsong. It was a wonderful place to meet with the Lord.

One morning I was praying. I didn't know how to pray. Should I ask for a church? Should I set aside the idea of ever pastoring again and just stay on the road? Should I ask for financial supporters? That morning, praying in the mountains, I sat in silence and talked to the Lord. Suddenly an answer came, swift and clear: "Just tell me that you will go where I want you to go and you will do what I want you to do."

It was so clear to my soul that I have never doubted it since. I would pray continually all summer, wherever I traveled and wherever I walked to pray: "Lord, I will go wherever you ask me to go. I will do whatever you ask me to do. I will say whatever you ask me to say."

There was a powerful sense of peace that came over my heart that morning out in the mountains of Kentucky, and it would return whenever I lifted my hands and my heart to God and repeated that simple prayer of consecration and surrender.

When I left the Kentucky Mountain Mission on Friday morning at the close of camp, the road followed a picturesque river bottom for miles. At one point, a bridge was out and the detour routed me up over a stark mountain road. My little Jeep faithfully climbed every steep hill and handled every sharp turn. It was hard that summer not to personify the little truck. He was so faithful. It was as if he were rising to the challenge ahead of us.

This afternoon as I write, thick snow has been falling all through the night, and I am taking advantage of a snow day to work on these stories. George is out there in the snow, faithful as an old horse. When I need him, he will be ready. Every couple of months someone stops by the place to see if he is for sale. I can't imagine ever selling him. He is like an old friend.

That summer day out in the mountains of the Daniel Boone Forest, my heart was full and tender from pouring out my heart to the kids all week. On the last night of camp, they told their stories around a roaring fire at the top of the hill where the camp sits. Their stories broke my heart over and over again and deepened my conviction of the need for the gospel among these beautiful mountain counties and all over the earth.

Driving like that you think. The summer of 2017 was the first summer in decades that Preacher Bill was not at the camp they call Youth Haven Camp there at Kentucky Mountain Mission.

Preacher Bill
On a previous visit to the Kentucky Mountain Mission, I was admiring the green beans one afternoon. I'd gone through the line in the dining hall and someone had put a serving of green beans on my plate. I felt like standing at attention. These were not salt-laden canned green beans packed in some factory. When you went through the line at the Kentucky Mountain Mission at breakfast, they would put a ladle of fried apples on your plate. Real. Fried. Apples.

At lunch or dinner they were likely to put on your plate a ladle-full of green beans that came from someone's home kitchen. These beans were snapped or "broke" on the porch and poured from a Kentucky woman's apron into a bowl and then cooked in a pressure cooker with bacon or pork and bacon grease and canned in a thick Mason jar.

One afternoon while I was enjoying my green beans, an elderly man sat across from me and introduced himself as "Preacher Bill." His name was Bill Holeman. His wife is Joyce. At the time, I did not know that across the table from me was a minister of the gospel as authentic as homegrown green beans. He was a legend in the mountain counties of Eastern Kentucky.

Preacher Bill grew up in California and went to the Los Angeles Bible Institute. He came to the mountains as a missionary in 1953 and began a ministry to children in the mountain schools. He has stories of telling stories in those schools. He had an old Jeep in the early days. He relied on

God and the goodness and generosity of God's people for rent and gas and milk for their babies.

Through all those years, God provided as Preacher Bill made his way from school to school and from church to church with the gospel for mountain children. He had two ventriloquist dummies, and in self-deprecating humor he referred to himself as "the dummy in the middle."

They loved him in those mountains, and he loved them. He lived with a smile on his face and his heart open to the children around him.

At lunchtime he told me an amazing story of a day when he had taken his Jeep up the wrong "holler" and stumbled upon someone's illegal moonshine operation...warning shots were fired in the direction of his Jeep, and he found his way out quickly and lived to tell the wonderful story for years.

Preacher Bill faithfully served his Lord, telling the story of Jesus to children in Kentucky for sixty years. He died on January 21, 2017. His testimony inspired me. I could not imagine a better way to spend your life.

As I drove away along the riverbed and over the mountains in my faithful Jeep, my heart was still filled with the stories of the campers. Their faces were in my mind.

One evening a young man came forward weeping hard. He told me that he had never met his dad. He had never seen a picture of his dad. When his dad left, his mother was so hurt that she destroyed any evidence of him. Weeping so hard that tears were running down his face, he said, "When I walk down the street in my town I look at men to see if any of them look like me, if they could be my father."

Like so many, I would leave the mountains and make my way north, but the mountains and the people would always be in my heart.

On the way out, I stopped at Chick-fil-a in Richmond for lunch. While I was there, I received an email from the chairman of the pulpit committee at Boone's Creek Baptist Church, near Lexington, only a few miles up the road. I drove by the church. It was a beautiful church near the Kentucky Horse Country. I told Lois. As much as she loves her Kentucky, we had promised the people at Bethel that we would be considered there. We told the people in Kentucky that we would have to wait to see if we were wanted in Jackson.

My next Red Jeep Journal entry was sent early in July.

A Stone for a Pillow
I'm spending the summer on the road, rarely sleeping in my own wonderful bed, in my own wonderful house, next to my own wonderful Lois, next to an industrial-size roaring fan she loves that drowns out the sound of crickets in the night air.

I find myself in unusual places. I carry my Wiggy Bag — my mummy sleeping bag — with me just in case. I never really know what it will be like when I pillow my head at night. Often when I lie down at night I repeat a little phrase to myself, and my heart is warmed at the thought of it: "The Son of Man had nowhere to lay his head."

Often Jacob comes to mind, and one night he had a vision of God coming and going from his life. He woke up transformed. He had a stone for a pillow that night, and he was far from home, but God was there and promised always to be with him.

Am I spiritualizing to see Jacob's pillow of stone as the dim foreshadowing of the one who would come who had nowhere to lay his head, this one whom millions would follow? For the sake of the Story we travel far from home with great joy in our souls and sleep in strange beds so others will have rest for their souls—the rest comes only from the one who had nowhere to lay his head.

Kyle and Ollie
Years ago, at Camp Barakel, I met Elizabeth Winzeler. She was a counselor there. I called our oldest son and told him to come up to camp and meet her. Today they are married and have three adorable boys: Kyle, Oliver, and Leland. I return to Barakel to preach this week, and Elizabeth will meet me in Lansing with Kyle and Oliver. They will spend the week with me at the camp where their parents met.

How wonderful to look back over our lives and see the hand of our good God. He is good. Never doubt it. Even when bad things happen to you, never doubt the goodness of God.

Sweet Corn, Watermelon, and Summer Camp
It's the season of watermelon and sweet corn and summer camp all over America. Have you ever thought that all over Canada and the United States, during the

summer young people gather under the preaching of the Word morning and evening — thousands upon thousands of them. After a day of swimming and horseback riding; paintball and high ropes and diving; "octaball" and ping-pong; handcrafts and snacks; and good food and friends, they quiet their hearts and sing and listen to preaching prepared to help them face this beautiful but broken world and know that God is for them and not against them. Pray every day for campers all over this grand and beautiful land.

Camp Barakel
July 7, 2017

CHAPTER THIRTEEN

WILLING TO DIE

Back to Bethel

On July 9, 2017, I was invited to speak at Bethel Church in Jackson, Michigan. Lois and Hope and I would drive out to Jackson County that morning for the service. We had been in conversations with the pulpit committee; this would be an interesting day. When you get west of Ann Arbor on the trip from metro Detroit to Jackson County, the drive gets especially beautiful.

That morning we were together. On most of my trips that summer I was alone with my thoughts and with the Lord. God was providing. God was supplying what we needed. God was using my messages and my writing and my conversations with campers and others along the way. In our hearts we knew that God was faithful and he would sustain us through the injustice and slander and misunderstandings.

When I speak to young people, I always remind them that when something bad is happening to one who loves God, God is doing something good. Like never before, God was reminding us of his sovereign power and his goodness. He is the blessed controller of all things. He turns evil things to a good purpose. He can be trusted. He will never leave us or forsake us.

The drive to Jackson County that morning was worshipful. We listened to worship music and we paused to give God thanksgiving. Out at Bethel we seemed to get along well, though some thought I talked a little faster than they would prefer. We would wait to see if they were interested in seeing us again.

A Glorious Unfolding

The situation was very hard on our whole extended family. We all felt mistreated, abused, abandoned, betrayed, slandered. Our grown children, now living in different places: Texas, Oregon, other parts of Michigan, hurt for us. They prayed and they helped when they could.

All of them wrestled with the injustice of it. One day I got a call from Holly, our oldest daughter, who lives out on the coast of northwest Oregon. She was weeping and wanted to tell of an experience she had earlier that day.

"Dad, I was driving my car and I was just feeling so angry and so hurt for what they did to Heidi and what they did to you. My heart was so sad. I was listening to the radio and a song came on I have never heard before...When I heard it, I just had to pull the car over to the side of the road and weep.

The song went like this:

> *Lay your head down tonight*
> *Take a rest from the fight*
> *Don't try to figure it out*

Just listen to what I'm whispering to your heart
'Cause I know this is not
Anything like you thought
The story of your life was gonna be
And it feels like the end has started closing in on you
But it's just not true
There's so much of the story that's still yet to unfold

And this is going to be a glorious unfolding
Just you wait and see, and you will be amazed
You've just got to believe the story is so far from over
So hold on to every promise God has made to us
And watch this glorious unfolding

The song was a powerful comfort to us at the time and an amazing thing to look back on now, since so much of what God was doing has unfolded...and it has been a glorious unfolding...

There is so much more of the story to tell. In my online journals I did not tell all that I was doing or where we were being considered because there were people who were so determined to hurt us and interfere with our ministry. But we were continually aware that if God was for us it did not matter who or how many were against us, and when his plan for us unfolded, it was going to be glorious.

Driving out to Jackson County, we wondered if God would lead us to minister there. During times of seeking God's direction over the years, I have always been encouraged by the words of an old song:

There must be a humble place somewhere
In God's harvest field so wide

Where I can labor thought life's short hour
For Jesus the Crucified

I've always loved to think of that. I have the heart of a simple traveling preacher or a simple village parson. I did not know which I would be at the time, but I never loved him more; I was never so full of zeal to serve him and to preach his Word. I was just staying happy in the service of the King until he made clear what was next.

My next Red Jeep Journal entry would include a couple of faith-strengthening stories. One of them was only beginning, but at the time we did not know that.

What's Next?
This weekend I am near home preaching on the Lord's Day. Next week, Hope America and I will be at Camp Barakel. This will be my third of four engagements this year at that "blessed place."

Here are a couple faith-strengthening stories:

How Can I Help You?
Last week at Barakel I was preparing to speak when I got a call from Lois. She was paying the bills and needed me to handle some details. We talked for a while about financial matters and concerns, and then we both agreed about how remarkable God's provision has been since we set aside a regular church paycheck.

A text came in just as I ended the call. It was from a friend , named Ed Creech who was inquiring about how he could be a help to us. He said he wanted to help us financially. Immediately, a monthly amount sprang into my mind. It was a generous amount, so I set the thought aside as wishful thinking.

"How can I help financially?" he texted.

"You can share a one-time gift or a regular monthly amount," I said, not mentioning the generous amount that had come to mind.

The next text shocked and delighted me. He wrote, "I was thinking...," and he texted the exact generous amount that had been on my mind. In a couple of days, that pledge showed up in our missionary account as a monthly promise and continued every month.

Another couple visited the Barakel chapel. When I checked my account earlier this week, I saw that they had also given a generous gift to our ministry. I wish I could tell you more of the stories of God's provision already this summer. It is remarkable and faith-building.

Let me tell you another story that will strengthen your faith.

Are You Willing to Die?
I had another amazing "providence of God" moment yesterday. Yesterday I was out in the yard stretching the July 4th holiday toward the end of the week. I was enjoying the cool breeze under the shade of a good leafy tree, and I called a friend who is going through a dark trial.

I said to him: "Tom, you haven't heard me preach for a while. Why don't I give you a little minute-message right now?"

"I'd like that," he said.

I explained to him how according to Revelation, the saints overcome Satan because of three things: the blood of the Lamb, the word of their testimony, and their willingness to die.

I explained that when we are ready to die with the praise of Christ on our lips, there is no trial so dark and deep that it can defeat us. A believer who is ready for the slaughter for the glory of God is already "more than a conqueror" in Christ. You cannot defeat one who is already willing to die.

Over and over again I emphasized, "Tom, if we are willing to die, nothing can defeat us."

Just then a van pulled up and the son of a friend got out of the car with a package for me. I excused myself from my phone call. My friend handed me a package. I stood in the shade of the tree and opened the box.

In the box were two books. On the top was a book with this exact title: *Willing to Die*. The shade under the tree in front of Granville Cottage was sacred ground yesterday afternoon when that book arrived.

I called my friend back, and we both rejoiced together. Before midnight I had read both books, and I went to bed with a powerful assurance that God is at work even in the darkest trials we face.

Granville Cottage
June 27, 2017

My calendar was full every Sunday and every week except the 9th of July. I had set that week aside to travel to Texas to meet our newest grandchild, Waylon Wesley, born to our son Daniel and his wife, Katelyn.

It was a hot week in Texas, but Dan and Kate's place had a pool. We spent every day in the pool—reading, swimming, being together, enjoying little Waylon, and we sampled local food in the evenings. It would be our last summer with Hope before she left for college. It would be our only week together all summer until my preaching was done in mid-September.

Daniel and Katelyn helped support us during The Red Jeep Journey. Along with a generous monthly gift, they sold me their late-model Toyota Camry that week, and I drove it home from Texas at the end of the week. Lois and Hope flew back to Detroit; I drove my new car, which I named Wilfred Grenfell after the great missionary adventurer.

In my personal journal that day, this is what I wrote:

I will drop the ladies off at the Houston airport at 6 p.m. and start north toward Michigan at that time. By midnight I should have six hours of the trip behind me and be near Little Rock, Arkansas. That would leave a fourteen-hour day of driving ahead of me on the Lord's Day, June 25. That is doable. I have made a reservation at a hotel that is a good value and should be fairly clean and safe. I will drive home with the Lord as my company on the Lord's Day. [I love you, Lord. I love you with all my heart. Thank you for all you have done for me. How could I ever thank you enough? You are my God and my King!]

I left Texas early Saturday morning, stayed overnight in Little Rock, and left early on Sunday morning for the long trip back to Michigan.

Toward late morning, I began to think about finding a church that morning. I longed to express my love and thanksgiving to God with his people somewhere along the way. As I drove, it occurred to me that this would be the only Sunday I was not preaching for the rest of the year.

Somewhere in southern Illinois, I found a church and pulled into the parking lot a few minutes before the service began. I slipped in and sat toward the back. I sang and prayed and thanked God in my heart over and over again for his provision, direction, and protection for our family during this time.

As I sat in this humble group of Jesus-followers, my heart was flooded again with gratefulness and love for God. I was not there to preach or serve. I was not there so much to be a blessing to others. I was not there especially for the message or what I could get out of it. I was there that morning with a deep desire in my heart to express my thanksgiving to God among his people.

> *"I will tell of your name to my brothers;*
> *in the midst of the congregation I will praise you."*
> Psalm 22:22, ESV

My next Journal entry described ministry in a place I had never been before.

The Red Jeep Journey Returns to Camp Barakel

When we passed the halfway point of the summer, I was speaking at Camp Barakel. Our daughter Hope was with me; she drove George the Red Jeep to and from Barakel. We left Barakel on Sunday afternoon after a rich week of ministry. We will return to Barakel for Family Camp on Labor Day weekend.

South of the Zilwaulkee Bridge and just north of Birch Run on the way home, we ran out of gas. We prayed, and a wrecker pulled up behind us immediately and offered to return after servicing another motorist in distress. Within twenty minutes, a black Jeep pulled up behind us and said: "Ken, what are you doing here? Do you need some help?"

We were over 100 miles from home, and the driver of the black Jeep was our neighbor and friend Paul, who lives directly across the street from our home in Granville Cottage. The blessing of God on the ministry this summer, his provision and protection, deepen our love for him and our confidence in him.

I finished preaching at Barakel on Sunday morning. On Monday morning I would leave for New York and then drive to Kentucky for a conference. Almost every day all summer I would preach twice a day and once or twice on Sunday. I would take Grenfell on the next leg of the preaching tour.

Camp in the Finger Lakes
Yesterday I spent most of the day on the road. By late afternoon I had arrived at Lamoka Lake in the Finger Lakes region of New York. The Finger Lakes are long, narrow, deep, north-south lakes in New York state, south of Lake Ontario. The camp is located in the peaceful country between the two westernmost lakes.

The speaker's cottage where I am staying this week has three rooms and a perfect porch and sits on a hill overlooking the camp and the lake. The chapel is on the highest point of the camp, facing down the lake from north to south.

I arrived in the late afternoon and had time to meet some campers and staff over dinner. The first chapel meeting is always a time when the campers are measuring the speaker a bit. They listened well, and I had time for a nice walk along the lake at sunset and an hour on the cottage porch watching the campers mingle, smelling the wood fire, and watching the afterglow out on the lake before bed.

New Roads
I will leave here on Saturday and take roads I have never taken on a seven hundred-mile drive through New York, Pennsylvania, and West Virginia into Eastern Kentucky. On Sunday I will preach at New Prospect Baptist Church in Manchester, and during the week I will speak for the pastors' meeting at Oneida Baptist Institute.

It is so encouraging every night to pillow my head with thanksgiving for what the Lord has allowed me to do this summer and realize that he has met our every need through the kind generosity of others. For those of you in The Fellowship of the Red Jeep who pray and give and follow our ministry, Lois and I and the family are deeply grateful.

Conner's Story
This week I've been in New York state. It's beautiful here. They build camps in beautiful places, but it doesn't take long to uncover the ugliness of sin just below the surface—even in beautiful Christian places.

The campers are a little more reserved here in New York than they were in Kentucky or at some of the other camps where I speak. After I open my heart to them, they tend to open their hearts to me. When they do open up, the story is often the same.

Commonly it's a story of the pain of having a parent who loves you, often a mother, who cannot break free of addictions. Sometimes the camper sits quietly after chapel and tells of the incarceration of his or her mother or dad, or they tell of a fractured home life due to drug or alcohol use. It is not uncommon at all for a camper to tell, like young Conner (not his real name) did last night, of his mother's death due to a drug overdose.

One boy wept as he told of never meeting his father and always wondering when he looks into the face of a man on the street if it could be his father. Another tells of his mother calling one night to say goodbye. He had said, "I'll see you in the morning," but he didn't because... after she got off the phone, she took her life.

My messages are filled with stories. Campers will frequently ask, "Can I tell you my story?" Conner stood quietly on the outskirts of my conversation with another and waited his turn; then he quietly said, "Can I tell you about how I met God?"

"It was when my mom died of a drug overdose. I think she took drugs because she was so sad she couldn't see us kids. I went to her funeral and I was looking at her in her casket. I didn't cry, but right then I knew God was telling me to follow him."

A storm had come through earlier in the day and power-washed the camp. It brought cooler air. We sat down on a bench and talked for a while in the cool evening. Conner told how he stayed alternately with grandparents and other relatives. He does not see his father much. He is only 13 and his mother is dead.

We prayed, and he thanked me for listening to his story. He said, "If it helps other kids follow God, you can tell my story." Then he went off to get a snack.

Camp will end today, and I may never see Conner again, but this camp will be here for him—a beautiful place where he comes every year. Here in sight of a pristine lake, kind people use Scriptures and songs and food and games and quiet conversation to show the beauty of Jesus to a young boy who has had to experience some very ugly things.

Lamoka Lake, New York
July 21, 2017

On The Red Jeep Journey, three things were always on my mind: Lois and Hope and the family back home with Heidi and her little ones, Keira and Koen, were always on my heart. I was not there with them, and things were difficult and sad and uncertain. My next talk was always on my heart, sleeping or awake; I was always thinking of the next message. The talks just kept coming at me, and they would until the 17th of September, but deep in my soul continually was a concern for provision.

God has been faithful to provide for our family down through the generations. I saw it firsthand growing up. I cherished stories about how the Lord provided for my grandparents. Lois and I continually experienced it. But now I was almost 60 years old. My previous ministry had taken a very hard landing. What church would want an older pastor so close to the usual retirement age? What would the future be like, and how would I pay my bills?

While I was in New York, I received a call from a camp in Michigan. They wanted me to speak for a men's retreat in the spring of 2018. They asked if the date was open. I did some checking. It was. I asked them to send me the details. That week in New York the speaker's quarters were in a little building with a nice porch looking out over the camp with a view of the lake. I thought about Hope and wondered if we would have to ask her to delay her time in Oregon at the Bible college. I thought about the tuition, the travel, the expense of a car. I wondered how we could do it.

Out there on the porch and as I drove along or walked the beach, when the burden hit me, I immediately obeyed the command "Don't worry about anything" by turning every

91

worry into a prayer request. I just kept trusting to God things that were out of my control.

Later that week I heard back from the Camp in Michigan that had asked me to speak. Their honorarium was unusually large. I would be paid enough in that one weekend of speaking to pay a third of Hope's tuition for the Bible college program. That night I called Lois and Hope, and we rejoiced in the goodness of God once again. Before Hope returned from Oregon after successfully graduating from the Bible school, we would have more stories to tell all along the way.

I preached Friday night at the camp, talked to some campers, and said my goodbyes, then packed and pulled away while the sun was coming up in the pink morning sky. It would be the longest drive of my summer; I needed to get an early start. I had promised to preach at the New Prospect Baptist Church in Kentucky the next morning.

I tell that story in my next Journal entry:

Journal Dictation in Pennsylvania
The first draft of this Red Jeep Journal entry was dictated while I sped down the highway in Pennsylvania.

I'm driving 710 miles today from New York through Pennsylvania, West Virginia, and Eastern Kentucky, along the old Hillbilly Highway and into Hazard and deeper into the mountains to Oneida.

Right now I'm in the beautiful Allegheny Mountains in Pennsylvania. I just passed Happy Valley, where Penn

State plays football. It put a smile on my face on this midsummer morning to think about cool autumn afternoons and Big 10 football. West of Happy Valley, the highway cuts through fold upon fold of beautiful blue-green mountains. The mountains are all crowned with white mist this early in the morning.

It's hard to describe how peaceful and compelling this landscape is. It deserves more time and attention than I have to give it today. I'm on a mission.

I just drove through a town called Shiloh, and it reminded me of a ballad by Andrew Peterson, so I looked it up on Spotify and now I'm listening to all the songs on Spotify named "Shiloh." Some of them are Christian songs; some of them are Civil War ballads.

I'm alone with my thoughts today, and so my thoughts are about the last time I visited Pennsylvania to preach. My friend Tom Harmon recommended me to a group of Brethren churches who brought me in for a united service as a preaching storyteller. I took Holly, Heidi, and Hannah with me to do children's work, sing, and keep me company. They put us up in a beautiful bed-and-breakfast called the McLean House, run by a fascinating literate Christian woman who made a delicious hazelnut-vanilla coffee and never let my cup get empty.

The bed-and-breakfast was beautifully decorated with antiques. The only thing out of place was a life-size cut-out of "Joe Pa" in the kitchen that would give you a start early in the morning when you came down tracing out the smell of coffee.

I get that familiar lump in my throat when I think back about that time with the girls. It ended up being a very happy memory for all of us, and we look back upon it with fondness. It was a simple assignment but a cherished memory.

As always, when I travel and preach I'm not sure what good I did, but I do know that the seed was good and I planted it well, and the rest belongs to God.

Tomorrow I preach to the people of New Prospect Baptist. Now I need to get to Oneida in time to prepare my soul with a thoughtful evening walk along the South Fork Kentucky River. I'll take a picture or two for you to enjoy in my next Red Jeep Journal entry.

Arrived in Hazard
I'm in Kentucky now, and today there was not a single stretch of 100 yards that was not a beautiful mountain scene. Seven hundred ten miles of unbroken scenic beauty; 710 miles of unbroken worship.

I miss Lois when I'm in Kentucky, especially. We talked on the phone a bit and remembered an evening together up on Natural Bridge at the restaurant overlooking the park. We ate Kentucky Brown and blackberry cobbler and coffee with ice cream for dessert. I vow to return with her one day, God helping me, and repeat the quiet evening together.

Hazard, Kentucky
July 22, 2017

Deep in the Mountains

I'm deep in the mountains of Eastern Kentucky, a region I have come to love. I've been traveling into these mountains every year for the last thirty-nine years. I've come to love the people and the countryside here.

On Sunday I preached at New Prospect Baptist. The church is pastored by my friend Dr. David Price. Sam Judd is his associate there. The church is out a road that is carved from a mountain, and it rests on the bank of a tree-lined, meandering body of water called Laurel Creek.

There are birdsongs here I have never heard before. It's good for a fellow's soul to quiet his heart and listen to birdsongs and take long, winding drives in the mountains and go to church on the banks of a creek. You should try it some time.

I am encouraging pastors this week at a mountain pastors' conference. My quarters this week are in a grand house on a hillside in the middle of a working farm. To get to the chapel, I can drive or I can walk the long route by way of the road, or I can walk across the farm, past the goats and chickens and over a swinging footbridge stretched over the river. I am a romantic at heart, so I usually walk.

Storytelling is natural to the people in these gentle hills. In the sessions I talk, but between sessions on breaks and over meals, I try to listen. I'm the featured speaker, but there are couples who have been doing ministry in these hills for decades. They have stories to tell and they often tell them well.

I'll tell you an interesting story I mined out of the hills of Kentucky a little later this week.

Oneida, Kentucky
July 24, 2017

Of Pigs and Moonshine Stills
So after a session yesterday, a cluster of mountain pastors was standing around swapping well-told stories. One of them was telling of a fella in his family who was good at woodworking.

Someone asked, "Did your dad teach you woodworking?"

"No."

"Well, where did you learn it?"

"I learned it in the pen."

"Why were you in the pen?"

"The Feds found my moonshine still."

"How did they find your still?"

"Well the hogs got loose and found it first, and they got drunk. When the Feds followed the hogs, they found my still, and then I learned woodworking in the pen."

I chuckled and thought to myself: "Now, that will make a great sermon illustration someday. I'm not sure what it illustrates, but I promise, it will make a good sermon illustration someday."

At lunch I ate with two mountain pastors. One of them had been in the ministry for fifty years. He and his wife had driven down the mountain road to Oneida to hear me. His wife said: "I'm looking forward to hearing you preach. You're handsome." She may have had failing eyesight, but she had a good, sharp wit.

Another man pastored one church for over thirty years. It was humbling to stand before them. They are kind people who love the Lord and the church and the ministry of the Word. They listened and responded with great interest and kindness. I found myself asking God for many more years of fruitful ministry if it would please him to allow it.

The music is being led by a giant of a man whose name is Jason Stewart, but everyone calls him "Buba." He used to drive for Dr. Al Mohler, the president of Southern Seminary. He would make a great bodyguard. He towers over me at 6' 7" and he is a big man, but he's not really a bodyguard; he is a musician—a worship leader and a very good one. He's doing a great job, and if he wasn't, I would never tell him so.

I'm sleeping well and eating well and enjoying my time in the mountains this week. The only thing wrong with this picture is that my little hillbilly wife is not in it this week. I will return with her, and we will dance at Hoedown Island and eat up at Natural Bridge and hold hands a little and drink some Ale 8 in cold, green glass bottles.

Oneida, Kentucky
July 25, 2017

CHAPTER FOURTEEN

LOVE AT FIRST SIGHT

The weekend of July 28–30 we were invited to return to Bethel Church to candidate for the pastorate. On Friday night, we would have time with the elders out at the Beasleys' place out on Cranberry Lake. We would have a meeting with the people on Saturday night with a Q and A time. We would have another Q and A time on Sunday morning during a combined Sunday School hour. I would preach on Sunday morning and drive home, and the congregation would vote on us that Sunday.

A Dark Question in the Bottom of My Soul

After my painful past experience, I doubted I would ever want to open my heart to a church again. The potential of hurt for me and for my family was just too great.

I have a theory that each of us has a dark question lying in the bottom of his soul. It's a lie or a half-truth. It has to be identified and understood, seen as the lie it is, and exposed. Truth must take its place for us to experience what God has for us. If we believe the lie and build our lives on the lie, it will destroy us. Jesus said of Satan, "The thief comes to steal, kill, and destroy." Satan is a liar and a murderer. His lies lead to the death of everything that is good and right and true and honorable and beautiful. But if we build our lives on truth, Jesus said that truth will set us free and give us life, even abundant life.

Because of painful bullying at school as I was growing up, this is the lie that lived in the bottom of my soul and haunted my thoughts late at night: "Ken, there is something about you that is unattractive and undesirable, and when people get to know you well, they will reject you. They will hurt you. Once they know you, they will not like you." This was not true, but it seemed true to me, and now that the people in my last church had gotten to know me for ten years, they were tired of me…The voice in my soul said: "When they really get to know you, they are going to beat you up. It's always been that way. It always will be."

Because I believed that lie, the idea of serving a new church was hard. When I drove out for the first interview, that dark thought returned: "Once they know you, they will hurt you. They will hurt your family."

"Maybe," I thought, "I will just treat it like itinerant preaching. I will go there and I will preach, but when they start to dislike me, they will hurt me. They will hurt my family. When I see that happening I will just leave before they can hurt us. I will keep this painful experience to myself, and I will hold the church at arm's length."

My resolve to do that dissolved when they asked me the first question: "Why did you leave your last church?" The whole sad story spilled out in that first meeting, and they listened with empathy. I opened my heart to them. They opened their hearts to me. They said Bethel is a place where I could heal. They were sympathetic about the sad circumstances of my departure. They asked me to return.

We returned on a delightful summer weekend. Instead of feeling like I had been put out to pasture, I began to see the potential of the church; I saw the heart of the church and found myself opening my heart to them. The church had a rich heritage and fine, sincere, thoughtful people who had been well taught. There was a genuine love among them. They were sound in faith and doctrine, but they were not petty and quick to judge. We began to fall in love with the church.

There was a clear moment when I gave my heart to the church. We were meeting with the pastors and elders out at the Beasleys' home on the lake. The food was good. The ladies had arranged a beautiful picnic and barbeque on the back deck under the shade of a huge tree overlooking a sweeping green lawn that ran out to the blue and silver lake. There was a slight breeze and the temperature was perfect.

We began to talk about church. We talked about what we believed church should be like. Over our food that evening, I began to see that this was a group of people I could not, I should not, I must not, hold at arm's length. I knew then that we had found our home, and I began to realize that we were not going to be put into an early retirement but were going to be invited into a time of great fruitfulness and flourishing for the Bethel church and for us.

The feeling must have been mutual, because we had been home only about an hour that Sunday evening when the call came from the chairman of the elders, Neil Veydt, that we had received an almost unanimous call to be the lead pastor at Bethel.

It was a happy day for us, and the future was coming into sharper focus. It was time to list Granville Cottage for sale and find a place in Jackson County to live. We had a mountain of work ahead of us: getting the house ready, finding a home, and moving our things, but on Monday morning Hope and I left for the Ohio Amish Country to speak at Skyview Ranch. Here was my journal entry that day:

The Ohio Amish Country
Hope and I will head to Ohio today to spend the week in the heart of Ohio Amish Country. I will be speaking to teens at Skyview Ranch this week. Next Sunday I will head up into the Michigan "Thumb" to preach at Deckerville Bible Church.

Pray for us, that campers would be saved and blessed and that I will not be tempted beyond that which I can bear by all the Amish baked goods within a short drive.

Skyview Ranch, Holmes County, Ohio
July 31, 2017

CHAPTER FIFTEEN

PROMISES TO KEEP

I wrote The Red Jeep Journal entry from Ohio Amish Country the next week:

Skyview Ranch

Hope and I are in Millersburg, Ohio. I am preaching to teens at Skyview Ranch. Skyview is in the heart of Ohio Amish Country. I have always loved this area. It has a wholesome feel to it.

The house where we are staying this week has a wide, shady porch, and Hope has spent hours there reading. We have had time for some drives in the Ohio countryside to see tidy Amish farms among the hills and to sample the local food and baked goods. It would not be good for me to come here often.

The weather has been perfect this week. We had a few showers yesterday, but I was taking a nap when they came. It may have rained in the night once, but the campers have enjoyed a picture-perfect week. I have been teaching the Book of Romans to the teens. It is a delight to have a week to teach a book of the Bible to young people and watch them drink in the truth.

A Delightful Surprise

Years ago we started a church not far from here. One day I called on a young man in the hospital who had rolled a cement truck. His name was Lewis. I led Lewis to Christ that night. His wife was there, and after I left she took the tract I had left with them and went to the hospital chapel and prayed to follow Christ. The next day, Lewis died. At the time, they had a little boy named Wes who was 4 years old.

Wes manages a restaurant not far from here, so he and his mother and a friend came to chapel to hear me preach last night. There is no joy like the joy of following Christ and making him known. Only God knows what will happen when we are faithful at that. After chapel, we all posed for a picture and my heart was full.

Skyview Ranch
August 3, 2017

After the week at Skyview I headed home overnight and left to drive up into the Thumb of Michigan on Sunday morning, early. On Sunday mornings that early, there is very little traffic, even driving through Detroit south to north. The sun was up. My soul was glad in the Lord. I had a church. Now I just needed to finish my preaching tour and once again I would be a pastor. After preaching at Deckerville and eating out with the Nutzman family, they dropped me off to spend the afternoon at the parsonage. I took a walk in the little village, enjoyed a nap, and then sat down to write the next entry for The Red Jeep Journal:

Radio on the Road

They build camps in remote, beautiful places. I've been on the road a lot this summer, driving to some beautiful places to speak at camps. On the road, I often drive along in silence with my prayers and thoughts. I also love to listen to a good podcast on the road.

When I was a boy, I loved radio—still do. Now we have "radio on demand," or podcasts. A good podcast is great company for a road trip. I still aspire to build a good podcast. In the last few years I have been experimenting with my own.

Adventure Deficit

Our son Kyle has a friend named Drew DeVries who has created a fine podcast called Adventure Deficit. You may have noticed that there will never be a time short of the New Heaven and the New Earth to take all the adventures we would like to take, but you can read about them and you can watch them on TV and, especially when you are on the road, you can listen to adventures on podcasts.

One of the podcasts was about the North Country Trail; another was about a father-son cross-country motorbike adventure along the Rio Grande from Colorado to the Gulf of Mexico. They celebrated by fishing for shark in the Gulf of Mexico, baiting them in kayaks. That episode was full of interesting stories.

Drew would invite me to tell the story of our North Manitou Island trip the next spring, but at the time I could not see that far ahead. It would have brought lightness to my heart if I could have seen into the future, to see what God would do, but he wants us to walk by faith, trust his promises, and leave the future to him. There was more to add to The Red Jeep Journal that Sunday afternoon:

Where Were You Fifty Years Ago?

What were you doing fifty years ago? I remember distinctly what I was doing: for the first time, I was a camper at Lincoln Lake. It was my very first summer camp.

I remember the chapel, which at the time was in a World War II-style Quonset hut building.

I remember the choruses we sang: "With Christ in the Vessel" and "I Know Who Holds the Future." (I sang with all my little heart, and I still love both those songs.)

I remember my counselor, who was a pastor.

I remember the burning question that I asked him about assurance of salvation.

I remember some trouble I had (it's personal) and...

I remember the nice nurse lady who helped me.

I remember swimming in the lake and playing "find your counselor" (he hid under a rowboat—nimble fellow).

This week when the campers gather in their chapel at Lincoln Lake, I will be their chapel speaker. I hope they have happy memories of swimming in the lake and sleeping in the cabin or yurt with their buddies. I hope they have a good counselor. I hope the camp songs still ring in their hearts after five decades have passed. I hope they cherish the sweet story of the Cross over the years as I do. I hope each of them is soundly and securely and sincerely saved and that fifty years from now Lincoln Lake will be a happy memory for them too.

Deckerville, Michigan
August 6, 2017

The next entry was written while I was at Lincoln Lake Camp. I wrote it in their beautiful second-floor dining room overlooking the lake. Coffee was on hand, and the joyful banter of campers and camp staff kept me company.

The Journey Goes International
This week I'm driving Grenfell. George the Red Jeep is still in the family and doing well, but God provided an opportunity for us to have a very late-model and efficient car for our ministry. I have missed George on some of our trips, but our new car, Grenfell, named after the great missionary to Labrador, Sir Wilfred Grenfell, has been a great blessing in our travels.

I will be heading up into the "Thumb" a couple more times in August for a summer Bible conference of Sundays at Deckerville Bible Church. I will return to Canada to a family camp up toward Georgian Bay for a weekend in mid-August, and then we will be heading up to Camp Barakel for Family Camp on Labor Day Weekend. I am scheduled to speak at a men's retreat at Pleasant Valley Bible Camp during the weekend of

September 8–10. I think there are still openings at Pleasant Valley, if you would like to join us.

The ministry this spring and summer has been more fruitful and fulfilling than anything I could have imagined, but this fall our schedule is even more exciting and full. You can learn where I will be preaching this fall by keeping your eyes on this website. All the details will be on the "Ministry" page when the time is right.

Until then, thank you for all you have done to keep me on the road preaching the Word every day all spring and summer long.

Lincoln Lake Camp
August 8, 2017

I wrote again from Lincoln Lake on Friday of that week:

Forty-One Years Ago Today
This morning as I prepared for the day, it occurred to me that it was forty-one years ago today, at the age of 17, that I was called to pastor the Pleasant Ridge Bible Church in Fort Recovery, Ohio. I started preaching when I was 14, so I have been preaching for forty-four years, but I started pastoring at 17 over forty years ago.

Summer Camps End Today
Today I will preach twice at Lincoln Lake and then head home to sleep in my own bed. I will preach in Deckerville this Lord's Day and head to Canada next weekend, but my summer camp preaching has come to an end.

A couple nights ago I sat overlooking the lake as the sun set. I watched the colors of afterglow on the lake and in the sky and my heart was warmed with thoughts of the faithfulness of God. He gave me favor with many camp directors and church leaders to fill my calendar every week and every weekend all spring and all summer long. It was a holy moment, and I poured out my thanksgiving to God for his great faithfulness. It was fifty years ago this summer that I first attended camp, and it was in this very place.

When I drive away from the men's retreat at Pleasant Valley Bible Camp on the 10th of September I will, by the grace of God, have preached 116 times this spring and fall. I have been to Michigan, Indiana, New York, Kentucky, West Virginia, Pennsylvania, and Ohio—oh, and Canada, eh? I will have preached in five states and two countries this spring and summer.

God's Provision—God's People
When I began in April, there were two questions on my heart: Will I have places to preach? Will I be able to pay the bills?

Well, the answer was yes and yes, thanks be unto God and those he has moved to help us. Not only have we preached almost every day, often twice a day, but we have been able to pay every bill. We have been very careful in our spending, and God's people have been generous to help us. Thank you to those of you who help us.

Big News This Fall
We have some very exciting plans this fall. Keep an eye on the kenpierpont.com website. Very soon, we will make a special announcement about our ministry this fall. You will not want to miss it.

Lincoln Lake Camp
August 11, 2017

Deckerville Bible Church

Every weekend of August but one I drove up into Michigan's Thumb to preach on the Lord's Day, morning and evening, at Deckerville Bible Church. This was a blessing to me and a very warm memory now.

I treated the assignment like a "summer Bible conference" and taught through the Book of Romans in six messages. I would arrive in time for the morning service, have lunch with a family from the church, spend the afternoon resting and writing in the church parsonage, and then drive down the "thumb of Michigan" toward home as the sun set after the evening service.

The afternoon meals were taken in homes, and they were wonderful farm-people meals with beef and chicken, corn and noodles, potatoes with real butter, pies and cakes, and garden produce. The conversations around the table were as rich as the food. These good people loved the Lord and his church. They loved the Word and had high regard for those who were ministers of the Word. I would not soon forget them.

Deckerville was a wonderful church filled with fine people. I loved them. They were good to me. It was delightful to spend most of the Sundays in August with them. Their Christian warmth and kindness still make my heart glow when I call them to mind.

I have one dark memory, though. I made the mistake of mentioning my love for carrot cake while I was there, and the people there, male and female, know how to make carrot cake. I walked away with not one—but two—carrot cakes, and these were heavy cakes with dangerous insulin-shock-inducing frosting. There are just some hardships you have to endure in ministry.

The Raven

On August 18–20 I drove into Canada to speak for a group that has often invited me to speak before. This was way up toward Georgian Bay in Ontario. The event was a nice three-day family camp. I left the Detroit Downriver region and drove to Port Huron on Friday in time to do a little shopping and have a late lunch before I crossed the Bluewater Bridge into Canada. I found Lois a gift in a quaint little vintage shop there and drove to The Raven for coffee and lunch before crossing into Canada. The Raven is a little coffee shop with a literary theme. It is built within sight of the water. It has a loft eating area and a small stage over the main door for an ensemble of no more than three musicians. The walls are lined with books. The menu is creative, and the dishes have literary names. The air is filled with the aroma of coffee; I believe they roast their own beans.

I order a corned beef and Swiss sandwich with a bowl of soup and had it served with loaded potato salad, which is potato salad with bacon and onions and other things so tasty you keep thinking of them halfway across the Bluewater Bridge into Canada.

I'd built into my schedule a margin of time to do some writing, so I took my bag and laptop with me. Within an hour I had crossed Lake Huron into Canada and I was on my way north and east toward the family camp.

Arriving in time to be prepared for the evening session, I began to unload my car into my comfortable speaker's quarters when I discovered that I had left my Bible, notes, iPad, laptop, and briefcase and everything in it back at The Raven, a three-and-a-half-hour drive away. I was thinking about the potato salad when I should have been thinking about the expensive tools and pricey electronic gizmos I was leaving behind.

I called. They promised to hold them until Sunday evening when I would come back through, but I had to borrow a Bible and preach completely from memory. The Lord helped me, and during the weekend we had a rich meeting. I was able to spend time with some families and couples between sessions, helping them work though life situations that were hard. I would like to believe I did some good among them. I believe my preaching and ministry that summer were stronger because I was preaching and counseling from a broken heart that was relying fully on Jesus for help.

Between sessions I ate with the families in small clusters around fires where they were camping out. The food was abundant and good. These people knew how to cook. The fellowship was rich. These people knew the Lord. When I was not preaching or spending time with the people, my own burdens would return. I was heartbroken for our daughter Heidi and her children and the unrelenting hardships she had to face. My soul was often heavy when I thought about her circumstances. I found myself often seeking God for his help for her and for her little ones, praying that God would work in the hearts of those who had hurt her, who had hurt us. I often wrestled in my heart for understanding about how to deal with the ongoing hurts, injury, and injustice of it all.

A week or so after I returned to the States we had a significant financial need related to our daughter's situation. We had no idea how to come up with the large amount of money we would need for her to continue to keep her attorney to defend her parental rights. That week we received a generous check in the mail from the group in Canada. Again, God has provided all that we needed just when we needed it. The attorney was worthless, but God and his people were faithful. (God would use a couple of attorneys in our lives in remarkable ways; keep reading.)

We were nearing the end of our summer ministry. I wrote again to The Fellowship of the Red Jeep:

The Summer of 2017
The sweet summer of '17 is coming to an end and I will never forget it. It really started on the 11th of April when I drove into the mountains of Kentucky to preach. The dogwoods and redbuds were just opening in the mountains. When I conclude my Red Jeep Journey on September 10th and drive away from Pleasant Valley Bible Camp, fall will be in the air and the trees will begin to blush with the first touch of autumn. I will have

preached 116 times this spring and summer and safely traveled thousands of miles.

Twenty-Six More Days

Last night I stepped out onto the street in the evening. It was cool and breezy. My good neighbor Brad was walking his dog and called out, "Feels kinda like fall." It does. In twenty-six days we will assume our full-time ministry with Bethel Church. Until then we have three more promises to keep and eleven more messages to preach up-state as autumn comes.

It was chilly on my walk this morning at dawn. The Lions play tonight, and it almost feels like fall. We are about 30–40 percent packed and getting Granville Cottage ready to be listed and officially offered for sale. Today a member of The Fellowship of the Red Jeep, Arlene Champnella, wrote and said she had set aside some boxes for our move. I jumped in George the Red Jeep and drove over to fill it up with boxes. Every gift, every prayer, every encouraging word, every text, email, and visit have played a part in the wonderful spring and summer of ministry that we are about to complete.

Arlene came out into the drive and said: "There it is. There is the red Jeep." We stood in Arlene's driveway and went over some of the stories of what had happened this summer that will likely never be written down. One story of kindness and opportunity and provision and ministry tumbled into another. We have had so many who have blessed us, believed in us, helped us, gifted us, hosted us, prayed for us, visited us on the road, written to us. It's been overwhelming. People that we least expected to give have given generous gifts, and every bill has been paid. How thankful we are.

Now it is time to move to our new place of ministry, Bethel Church in Jackson. We have had offers to help move (that is how you know who your friends really are).

Hope America will head to Cannon Beach, Oregon, in October for Bible college. She is our baby. We are thrilled for her, but her absence is going to be an adjustment. Hazard is not going to know what to do with himself. Lois will be without her little buddy. I will cry. (I cry a lot. It's how I roll). I will cry that happy cry that means you have someone in your life you deeply love. Only deep love can make you cry like that. It's a bittersweet kind of thing.

Hope America is 18 now. When she turned 16 her mother wrote a tribute to her that was beautiful. This evening Hope and her mother are out on an errand. I thought you might like to read that tribute:

"When I realized I was pregnant in 1998, I already had 7 kids at home and the youngest was about 3; I had my hands full and running over. Ken and I had already decided years before to allow the Lord to give us as many kids as He wanted us to have so I was a little fearful. I was getting older; I was going to be 40 years old. But I knew God had given us another baby and He knew what was best for us; He knew the future and what we needed.

"Today as I write this I can't imagine what life would be like without our little Hope America. She is a delight to our souls. When she was born the other kids adored her, always playing with her so much so that she walked at 8 months. Now that the kids are all married or moved away for work, she is my little shopping buddy, she is my photography partner, let's-get-a-bite-of-lunch-buddy, craft store buddy, my sit-in-church-with-me-buddy. I can't imagine life without her. I love her so much.

"I know I can trust God; even when I am being selfish and think I have too much on my plate, and I can't possibly take one more thing, God is the one who sees the future and knows what I need in my life. Children are a blessing just as God told us in **Psalm 127:3-5:**

"Behold, children are a heritage from the Lord, the fruit of the womb a reward. Like arrows in the hand of a warrior are the children of one's youth. Blessed is the man who fills his quiver with them! He shall not be put to shame when he speaks with his enemies in the gate."

Thanks for being a part of the red Jeep team...

Granville Cottage
August 25, 2017

Chapter Sixteen

Mission Accomplished!

Lois and Hope and I would go to Barakel for the Family Camp on Labor Day weekend. We drove up together, listening to the radio. There was a song that comforted us in all of our turmoil over the last year, in what we were forced to go through, in all that our daughter was unjustly suffering. The song was based on the answer the young men in Daniel gave when they were commanded to bow to a false God or be burned alive. They said, "Our God can deliver us, but even if he does not, we will not bow."

Lois asked me to play the song, and we all wept at the goodness of God and his provision, protection, and direction in this dark season of our lives. He was faithful. He kept his promises. He did not shelter us from danger and betrayal and abuse and slander, but he was with us. He did sustain us. He provided for us. One group of people had abused us and treated us shamefully, but they did that to Jesus. He arranged for another group of people to open their hearts so us.

As long as I live I will cherish the memory of driving into the piney north country of Michigan playing that song over and over and over and weeping and thanking God for delivering us from the furnace. We were headed north to tell families that they can build their lives on the promises of God.

We were nearing the completion of our mission when I wrote this entry:

Labor Day Weekend Family Camp at Camp Barakel

On Labor Day weekend, Lois and I took Hope and headed up to Barakel for the weekend. I spoke for the Family Camp this year. It was a beautiful weekend— cool and sunny. In a month, Hope America (our baby) will leave for Bible school in Cannon Beach, Oregon, and our nest will be empty—except for Hazard, the Wonder-Yorkie.

Pleasant Valley Bible Camp Men's Retreat

This weekend I will head north of Torch Lake and Traverse City to Pleasant Valley Bible Camp in East Jordon, Michigan, for a men's retreat. On Sunday, September 10th, I will drive home, thus completing the sweetest summer of my life—a summer of unbroken ministry and travel to beautiful places of ministry— mountains and lakes and forests, camps and churches large and small. I met many hundreds of wonderful people and will have preached over 116 times. God met every single need.

Granville Cottage Is for Sale!

For the last ten years, Granville Cottage has been our home (it was named after the Old Granville Place on *It's a Wonderful Life*). Now we will sell it and buy a home near Bethel Church. Please pray for the quick sale of our home and purchase of a new home and our move if you think of us.

In a little over ten days we will assume our full-time ministry with Bethel Church. We are amazed, and we are grateful for all of you who have so faithfully helped us. Our souls are filled with joy, and our faith is strengthened. We will never forget the spring and summer of 2017.

Granville Cottage
September 6, 2017

This was my final entry in the Red Jeep Journal:

My Itinerant Ministry Is Complete
This weekend I am preaching at Pleasant Valley Bible Camp near the northern mouth of Grand Traverse Bay. It's a beautiful place. The weekend has been fall-like. The weather has been perfect. My quarters are comfortable. The furnace kicked on each night, and I think it may have frosted last night. The sky is clear and my heart is joyful in God.

My friend Jason Cross came with me this weekend and we have enjoyed rich fellowship. In a little over an hour I will preach my last message here and my last message of the summer—message #116 this summer.

On to Bethel
Next Sunday will be my first Sunday at Bethel Church in Jackson, where I have been called to serve as their lead pastor. I will bring The Red Jeep Journal and The Red Jeep Journey to a close.

Thank you to all of you who have been so faithful in helping us have a delightful summer of ministry all over the Midwest and into beautiful Canada. Our hearts are full and joyful and our faith is stronger than ever in our lives.

What Is Next?
Since we will no longer be publishing The Red Jeep Journal, we have a few other projects that we will be working on as a ministry and as a gift to each of you. Our messages will be live-streamed and archived from Bethel soon, so you can watch them if you like and share them with others. I have some ideas for a video podcast and some other ideas for writing and creating encouraging content to edify and encourage you.

Camp Lessons
Tomorrow morning I will begin releasing short videos that I call "Camp Lessons." I will post the videos once a week for the next fifty weeks: *50 Lessons from Camp*. In the videos I will share truths that I have shared with both campers and retreat participants this summer in a brief video format. You can easily share the videos with others via social media. I hope they will remind campers of things they learned this summer and spread truth to others who were unable to attend camp.

Pleasant Valley Bible Camp
September 10, 2017

Hope left for Bible college in Oregon in the fall, and Lois and I were left alone to prepare the house for sale. Until Granville Cottage was sold, we could not buy a place in Jackson County. We had a lot to do to prepare the house; there were inspections and repairs to complete. We eventually would replace the whole roof before the house sold.

My brother Kevin and a couple of his boys, Zachary and Josiah, spent a couple days helping us get the house ready. A friend named Dennis spent many hours helping get the house up to code to pass the city inspection. One bitterly cold night, an old friend named Jason came over and stayed with me to help me haul things out of the basement. He worked hard and was good company.

On the night I called him for help, I was so weary. "Would you come over to help me move some things?"

I loved his answer: "Sure, Pastor. I would love to spend some time with you." I will always cherish Jason's kindness. At the end of the evening we ordered a pizza and feasted and stood praying before he left on that cold winter night. He had been a great help to me.

During The Red Jeep Journey, twenty-two different families gave us gifts. We emptied our emergency reserve and our retirement to pay our expenses and defend our daughter in court. When The Red Jeep Journey ended, the gifts and honorariums stopped coming in. My salary from the church would not begin for another couple weeks. It was exactly at this time that Hope needed funds for school, and we gave her our last $1,000 to buy a used car when she got to the West Coast.

Lois and I lay awake early one morning in October. We had paid the last payment on the shop. We had to pay a repairman to fix the air conditioner. We had no money. The church had given us a generous gift basket filled with gifts cards to every imaginable restaurant in Jackson. We used those to eat, but we now had no cash.

We had listed some furniture items for sale on Facebook Marketplace. There we were in bed on that Saturday morning, thinking about the money. We had almost made it. Our bills were paid. Our shop lease was paid. We were lying there talking about what we were going to do when the phone rang. A woman was calling about some furniture we had listed for sale. She came over and gave us cash. We were able to go to the shop and pay the repairman with cash.

"Well, praise the Lord. He has provided again," I said when I got back into the car with Lois. We are free of the lease now. We are almost there. Shortly after that, Hope called to tell us a couple had given her a used Honda Civic. She would be sending the money back. We were going to make it. We had $1,000.

When Hope's school term was finished and she graduated the next May, we still needed to pay her final school bill. We offered to give the car back to the couple who had given it to her. They said, "It belongs to you."

Hope drove the car until she graduated. She had one more school payment to make. Her brother Chuk found out about the debt and called the school. He paid her bill and then called her and said: "Your bill is paid. When you graduate, sell the car and send me the money."

The car sold for $1,000. Chuk called it even, and Hope graduated with her bill paid. We never missed a meal. God supplied everything we needed—every dime right on time. We flew out to Oregon to attend Hope's graduation, walked the beach, enjoyed the coffee, and savored the fellowship with our oldest daughter, Holly, her husband, Jesse, and our wee grandson Aiden Redemption.

When I get out to the coast, I love to walk the mountains or the beach or even the riverfront in Astoria. It's a place of shocking beauty. One sunny day I indulged in a couple of book shops, took a long walk on the beach, and then drove to a coffee shop recommended by our daughter Hannah and her husband, Dale. Sitting in the little car in the sun, I was overwhelmed with the goodness and favor of God, that he would have allowed us to face such a difficult time: such slander, injustice, misunderstanding, mistreatment, and hardship, and yet provide for us and protect us. Our daughter was still able to travel to Oregon, complete her course of study, have all of her needs met, have a car to drive, and graduate with all of her bills paid.

The Crowning Favor of God
During this time, God seemed to continually show his favor in unmistakable ways. Let me give you an example that will always be precious to me. Ed and Sunday came to our church years ago (the church where I had pastored for ten years before going to Bethel). They had been a couple for years, but they were not married. We had invited their daughter to attend church, and they began to attend too. God began to work in their hearts, and they began to follow the Lord. God had set them free from destructive habits. Their lives were completely turned around and they began to follow the Lord and seek the Lord.

Soon they called to offer to help us as a part of The Fellowship of the Red Jeep. They supported us faithfully and generously. We were grateful. I was disappointed that I had to leave my previous church before I had baptized them. I was sad that they had not yet married. Whenever I would meet Ed for breakfast, I would remind him that marriage was the next step.

To my surprise, Ed and Sunday showed up at Bethel. I thought it was nice to have them there as visitors sitting in the front row, just like they used to do at our previous church. The next week they came back, and every week after that. One day I said, "Ed, if you and Sunday are ready to marry, I will marry you."

"You will?" They were so glad. One summer night a few weeks later, we met in the little village of Chelsea and had BBQ and talked about their wedding. We stayed until they closed the place down. Ed and Sunday wanted me to know how completely and profoundly God had changed their lives since they had begun to follow him. They were deeply grateful for my ministry to them.

When I drove away that night my heart was so full. I thanked the Lord aloud. Over and over again God was using me. He was not done with me.

A few weeks later I drove over to do their wedding. I got a nice big coffee on the way and managed to spill about half of it on my white shirt. When I got there, Ed took one look at me and said: "What happened to your shirt? Hold on; I have an extra."

Why he had an extra shirt that fit me perfectly we could only attribute to the kind humor of God's providence that day. I performed their wedding in a little outdoor court where Sunday's mother was staying…though she had to watch on a video because she had been admitted to the hospital. A family of ducks waddled into the wedding party just as I was pronouncing them husband and wife. It was a happy day.

A bit later I would return and minister to Sunday's mother and then return to preach her funeral. In just a few weeks, it was my privilege to baptize Ed and Sunday at Bethel Church. There was great rejoicing in the church that day. None of the people was more joyful than Ed and Sunday.

Ed and Sunday moved from Romulus to Ypsilanti. They still drive a long way to Bethel every week, and they are members—faithful, joyful, serving members. Every Sunday, if I need a reminder that God is still using me, I just look down to the end of my pew during the singing, and there stands Sunday: delivered from alcohol and drugs, a married Christian woman, a godly grandmother with her little Charlotte there every week, hands raised in praise to God.

I will always believe that God looked upon Ed and Sunday and called them to himself. When he did, he encouraged a brokenhearted pastor who needed to know that he was still being used of God and showed a church the power of the gospel to transform people's lives.

My heart is so full when I realize that there are many, many hundreds of others like Ed and Sunday who live just a few minutes from our church, and if we are faithful God will use us, even when our hearts are broken.

PART TWO:

THE BITTERSWEET FARM JOURNAL

CHAPTER SEVENTEEN

A GOLDEN OCTOBER

When I finished The Red Jeep Journey, The Red Jeep Journal ceased to exist. I announced that I had new plans for the mailing list. We would call it The Bittersweet Farm Journal. In this section of the book, I will include some writings from The Bittersweet Farm Journal and I will fill in some details. I think you will agree that it's quite a story.

Here is the first entry: This is one of the sweetest and most remarkable stories I have ever written. I trust it will build your faith and encourage your heart.

Is God in It? Does It Have Character?
On July 30, 2017, I was called to pastor Bethel Church of Jackson, Michigan. When we knew we were moving to Jackson County and would be buying a new home, there were two things I wanted especially. We could do without either one, but I thought it would be good if these two things were true about the house.

One, I wanted to know that God was in it.

Two, I wanted the house to have some character, some uniqueness.

Neither of these things had to be true. God would be in it even if we did not have the luxury of a mystical sense of divine circumstances, and if the house didn't have special character, it would when Lois was done adding her touches to it.

The first day of October was a Sunday. After church, we would look for a house. The sky was clear and the air was cool that day. By the time we finished lunch and started our house-hunting it was late afternoon.

The first house was in a subdivision southwest of town in Summit Township. The drive out to the house took us down roads arched over with trees full of autumn color. The road rose and fell gently as we drove. One road had a small patch of trees along both sides of it. Just beyond the trees was a pretty, white farmhouse: beautifully maintained, yard groomed, grass green, sitting in a cluster of walnut trees. A little hand-lettered sign in front said, "For Sale by Owner."

"Look at that house," I said. "It's for sale by owner."

It was "the golden hour" of day. Sunlight slanted through the trees. There was a beautiful haze along the ground out in the field behind the house. The fields were framed with trees in the color of autumn. The sky was October-blue.

Lois said: "It's an old farmhouse. I'm sure it needs a lot of work. That would not be good for us."

"We have to take a look; it's a John Sloane house," I said.

A John Sloane House

For years I have enjoyed the paintings of John Sloane. Sloane often paints country scenes. Usually they have farmhouses in them. This house looked like it could have come out of a John Sloane painting. Behind the house was a field stretching back to a wooded area a half-mile away. Beside the house was a beautiful deer preserve. The hill directly across from the house was covered with woods. I circled back.

The owner, a man named Charles, was kind and eager to show us his place. It was beautifully and tastefully restored throughout. Parts of it were brand-new and other parts were beautifully restored. It had new windows, driveway, roof, furnace, air, bathrooms, and kitchen. It was charming. It was painted white, had a little two-story barn beside it, and sat on a delightful two acres of land.

After our tour, I asked Charles if he would consider an offer contingent on the sale of our home. He immediately agreed. We agreed on a price. He included all the appliances and a number of valuable possessions and upgrades. We went home hopeful. The house certainly had character—but was God in it? Would he allow us to have this delightful place? As Lois, Hope, and I drove away, we prayed that God would allow us to have this home if it was his will.

Charles called a few days later and promised to hold the property for us until our house sold. He took the house off the market and didn't entertain any backup offers. He promised to save the house for us. He was true to his word. He moved out on December 15. Granville

Cottage sold on January 16, and we bought the home on January 19 and moved in on the 20th.

A Name for Our New Home

At Thanksgiving, Wes and Dylan, Dan and Katelynn visited. Wes and Dylan were able to stay through Sunday. They visited Bethel Church, and we drove them out to the house to see it. While we were exploring, we came upon a patch of bittersweet growing in a fencerow. Lois loved to use bittersweet in decorating. When the children were young, we would drive the backroads in Ohio watching for bittersweet growing along the roads. It was always delightful to happen on a patch of it. Once, I remember stopping near Millwood, Ohio, and filling the back of the van with the stuff so Lois could make crafts and wreaths and help put food on the table. Searching for bittersweet was a happy memory.

That afternoon Lois and Dylan got out and cut a sprig of it. When they returned to the car, I knew immediately we had a name for our home.

The last few months had been very difficult—the most difficult months in our lives. Our hearts were broken. We had endured a dark and bitter providence. I had stepped away from our pastorate of ten years. Our circumstances were sad, but our God was faithful. People rallied around us to support us. Family members rose up to help. Camps and churches invited me to speak—over 116 times in the summer. From April to September my schedule was completely full. God protected us. God provided for us. God met all of our needs.

We would never forget The Red Jeep Journey and The Fellowship of the Red Jeep. It had been a powerful and unforgettable adventure. The people we met, the places we traveled, the meals we shared, the messages we preached, the needs that were met, the stories we shared, and the stories we heard all contributed to a priceless experience that would powerfully strengthen our faith in God and deepen our love for him. All of them rose up in a powerful testimony that God will keep his promises. You can trust him. He is faithful.

In July God gave us a fine church. Bethel Church allowed me to finish my speaking obligations, which I had booked into the second week of September. They allowed me to commute until Granville Cottage sold.

When Something Bad Happens to You, God Is Always Doing Something Good

When I spoke that summer, I often told the teens, "For those who love God, when something bad happens to you, God is always doing something good." During the season of trial, the sovereign power of God was a great comfort to us. We knew God was doing something good. We were willing to suffer misunderstanding and loss, but we would never doubt the goodness of our God.

Now with this sprig of bittersweet in my hand I thought of another beautiful and poetic way of expressing the same thought—another way of saying the same thing:

> *"When something bitter happens to you,*
> *God is doing something sweet."*

We made up our minds. If God would give us this little "farm," we would name it "Bittersweet Farm," because we never want to forget that when something bitter befalls one of God's own, he is doing something sweet.

Tonight I'm writing this story in a quiet corner of an upstairs room in the little place on the earth God has given us that we call Bittersweet Farm. It is our own, and we are making our life here in the beautiful countryside a few minutes from our beloved Bethel Church. Deer and wild turkey graze out behind our house, and the place is noisy with birdsong and bursting with beauty. It's our place on the earth.

Bittersweet Farm
January 26, 2018

CHAPTER EIGHTEEN

IT'S NOT A BARN

When we moved onto Bittersweet Farm I began to send my subscribers a weekly story and a bit of news about what was happening with the family and the ministry and Bittersweet Farm. The next few chapters are some of the stories of Bittersweet Farm. They are beautiful stories, but God was not done. There was something even more remarkable that would happen, even bittersweet, but first these stories:

A Delightful Discovery

When we moved to Jackson County in mid-January, I kept gently correcting people when they called our outbuilding a garage. I would smile and say, "Oh, that is not the garage; that is the barn..."

Last week Keith Gillmore came to service our central air-conditioning. Keith and his family have been part of the Bethel Church for years and he is a lifelong Jackson County resident. He told me that from the time he was 14 to 18 years old, he lived and worked in a cider mill. He had some fascinating stories to tell. Then he looked up at the barn and said, "That is a neat old carriage house."

"What? What did you say?"

"You have an old carriage house—a coach house. The carriage went inside that door," he said, pointing to the door, "and the horse went in the back. That is why you have the sliding barn door in back opening to the pasture. Originally, where the stairs go up to the loft there was only a ladder built against the wall so you could reach the horse's feed in the loft."

That made my day. We don't own a garage. We don't own a barn. We own our very own carriage house right here on Bittersweet Farm. This was a delightful discovery. I knew the building had been erected in 1920, but I hadn't realized it was a carriage house or coach house.

It has a sliding door on the northwest side. It has an overhead door opening to the drive on the east, and originally it had a sliding barn door on the north that would have opened into the barnyard or pasture. Now it has a stairway and a workshop built under the stairway, with a window in the workshop opening to a beautiful view to the north. It has a nice wood-burning stove and a good set of speakers installed by the previous owner.

Years ago, a friend, Gary Mickle, as a gesture of love, built me a stout set of shelves made from concrete forms. There are five indestructible units. They have been with me wherever I have gone since he built them for me about thirty years ago. They are a treasure to me, and now they line the north wall of our very own carriage house to organize our tools and supplies.

The carriage house is white, matching the farmhouse on Bittersweet, and it has a black standing-seam roof. It is a practical and handsome outbuilding with some character and history. The loft has windows opening to the east and west.

In future summers, I can imagine sleeping with the grandchildren in the carriage house loft. I will hang on their words and listen to their laughter and their joyful banter. Maybe I will fill the loft with the sound of the harmonica before we pray, and then we will drift into the sweetness of sleep with country sounds and country smells all around us. Maybe the light from the rising moon will fall on the floor of the loft while I tell them my stories.

Out in the distance the scent of skunk and the sound of crickets will be on the night air and maybe even the fragrance of newly mown hay—or the call of the barred owl from the woods across the road or the frightful sound of a bobcat...who knows? When you're sleeping in the loft of a one hundred-year-old carriage house, you never know.

What Happens When You Listen
I like to get to know the Bethel people so I can pray for them. I try to pray for every member and every attender every week. When I pray for them I try to discover their stories. When you get to know people's stories, it's easier to love and pastor them. It's also very common, when you are listening to people, for them to tell you things you never would have known. Sometimes you unearth valuable gems. Almost everyone has them if you listen well.

If I had not listened to Keith, I might never have known that we were the grateful owners of an authentic carriage house. In two years we will celebrate its centennial birthday.

Out in the drive, I watched Keith drive away in his shiny red truck and stood a little taller. With a simple story he had dramatically raised the poetic value of our home and raised the worth of our already priceless Bittersweet Farm.

Bittersweet Farm
July 11, 2018

CHAPTER NINETEEN

A PROPHETIC WORD

I believe when God is going to do something, he puts a prayer burden on the heart of a believer and he acts in answer to prayer. For this reason, it is a good idea for each of us who love the Lord to have an awareness of our desires. David wrote, "Delight yourself in the Lord and he will give you the desires of your heart."

When I go back through my writing and my journals, when I think back on our drives in the countryside, I realize that from my earliest days as a boy, God placed in my heart a powerful longing for the countryside. At the time, I didn't know why. Now I think I do. This was from an early Bittersweet Farm Journal entry:

> Here are a couple of paragraphs from an essay I wrote in about 1994 when we were living near Apple Valley in Knox County, Ohio, just off State Route 3. (Route 3 is a beautiful stretch of road that angles northeast from Mt. Vernon to Loudonville through Jellico and Amity and some of the most serene country in Ohio.)
>
> "I am privileged to do the pastorate along rural lanes and countryside and in quaint villages and small towns.

My parish is a beautiful one. This time of the year the gentle hills and glens of Knox County are ribboned with ripening crops and rich with the colors of autumn.

"Robert Frost wrote of 'being versed in country things…,' and that is an ambition of mine. I love the old places in the country best. Bank barns and big family homes back long, tree-lined lanes. Houses with character and a history. Not cookie-cutter track-houses but unique homes with their own personality and atmosphere."

I wrote that so many years ago. Since then we have lived in a beautiful parsonage; a large chunk of the sixth floor of a sixteen-story, four hundred-room conference center, and in a subdivision (ten years) —but now— since January of 2018, an old house with character and history with a century-old carriage house and a grove of walnut trees. The property is shared with birds and beasts and things that grow…

Ministry has always been the priority, and I continually consecrate myself to the service of Christ, but God chose to give us this little home in the country—a quiet place, a place almost exactly like the ones I wrote about in 1994.

Bittersweet Farm
July 14, 2018

CHAPTER TWENTY

THE TIME OF TIGER LILIES

On Sunday evening I returned from camp. One of the Bethel faithful was on his deathbed, so before I went home I drove to see him. He lives in the beautiful countryside northeast of the church. On the drive out to his house, the road was lined with banks of tiger lilies blossoming, bending forward, waving in the breeze — bright orange in the golden hour as the sun angled down the sky.

Last summer I lived in a suburb of a major city, but I was blessed to travel to Kentucky Mountain Mission to speak. The drive from Michigan to Kentucky follows an interstate highway, but an hour and a half from the camp I exit the interstate and travel through some of the quaint small towns and villages of the Bluegrass. Within an hour of the camp, I am in the mountains of Eastern Kentucky. I drive through the small city of Irvine, the county seat of Estill County, which sits in a valley on the Kentucky River. I cross the bridge in George the Red Jeep and make my way along a road that follows Miller's Creek and Big Sinking Creek through the valley all the way to camp.

That scene came to mind when I saw the explosion of tiger lilies, because last summer along the Big Sinking Creek, thousands of tiger lilies brightened the way that followed the river. There in my Jeep, turning along the roadway following the water running over rocks, I gave thanks to my God aloud that he would send me on such a mission in such a beautiful place. I did not know that less than a year later I would leave the bland suburbs behind and live in such a place.

The Year Before
The year before, I had spoken at the Kentucky Mountain Mission staff conference. They invited me to speak at camp. I returned in the summer and spoke to the teens. I was so warmly received by the young people. My friend Sam Judd was there, and it was a reunion and time of rich fellowship with him. A number of the teens began to follow Christ the week I was there. There were two young ladies who had trusted in Christ to be saved during my first year as a speaker; they greeted me joyfully when I arrived for my second year of speaking. They reported a year of spiritual growth.

When I left the camp at the end of the week, I followed the beautiful path along Big Sinking Creek, but the road over Miller's Creek was closed. A detour routed me over a high mountain in the Daniel Boone National Forest. It was a beautiful detour, and my heart was full and glad. I prayed grateful prayers as I drove my faithful red Jeep over those mountains.

I had some business in Irvine, and then I drove to Richmond to get gas. I always feel melancholy when I have to leave the mountains and join the great stream of traffic on the interstate flowing north. While I was thinking of the sweetness of a week of ministry, I checked my phone and found this entry on Facebook posted by one of those girls; her name is Brooklyn:

> So today is my spiritual birthday and I can't explain how much has changed since then. Before I was saved it was so hard to have joy and just be happy. But last year on this day (which was a Thursday last year) I was in chapel at Youth Haven Bible Camp listening to Ken Pierpont speak in chapel and it has truly changed my life. Ever since then I have been so happy and continuing to grow in my relationship with God. Being saved is the most important decision any person could make, it is truly life changing. Pastor Pierpont told this story about people who were just so low at life and was addicted to drugs and alcohol, and when they got saved their life got totally flipped around. Pastor Pierpont also made the reference that when you use a paddle boat it's so hard to get it going and continue to make it move. But when you are a Christian it's like using a sailboat, all you have to do is put up the sail and God will provide the wind.

That is what came to my heart on Sunday evening when I saw banks of orange lilies in the ditches bending toward the road along the way. My heart was filled joy at the power of the Story of stories and the great privilege it is to tell it to young hearts.

Bittersweet Farm
June 2018

CHAPTER TWENTY-ONE

THE CALL OF THE BARRED OWL

A month ago I sat down in the evening to make a journal entry. I want to share it with you in this edition of The Bittersweet Farm Journal:

> Tonight Hope made dinner. I had worked at the church and worked in the yard. Lois was returning from a trip out of town, and we timed dinner for her arrival.
>
> Hope piled the table with BBQ chicken, new red potatoes and butter, slaw, and corn on the cob.
>
> The corn was the first of the season, tender and sweet and with real butter and salt and pepper, a delicacy. It's as if the winter numbs your taste buds and the new corn of early summer awakens them. (Sometimes eating can be idolatry—on this evening, it was worship.)
>
> After doing the dishes we moved out to the "evening porch" to read while Lois puttered among the flowers.

It is May 29th. A year ago tomorrow I drove into Jackson to meet with the pulpit committee for the first time. Now, a year later, we have made our lives here and live in our little farmhouse right on the border of Summit Township and Spring Arbor Township, where when evening falls we sleep to the sound of the barred owl calling from the woods across the road.

Camp Barakel
June 30, 2018

The Sunrise Porch and the Evening Porch
A week from Sunday it will be July, and no summer in my life has ever flown so swiftly past. Next week I will make a holy pilgrimage to preach at Barakel. This week all the children are coming in. This is a rare and wonderful thing. We have a family wedding on Friday in South Bend. On Saturday the plan is for the whole clan to enjoy a walk out to the Grand Haven Light for sunset as we described in my first book, *Sunset on Summer*.

Out here on Bittersweet Farm it is impossible to describe the beauty of the month of June. The day begins when the sun rises over the trees east of the farm. The trees are all wearing their canopies of rich green, and the countryside is covered with growing things. The grass grows swiftly. Keeping Bittersweet Farm isn't really farming, because our only crops are grass and flowers and our only livestock is Hazard, the Wonder-Yorkie. Keeping the farm is a little more like grooming a park, but it's a delightful hobby and rewarding and a good excuse to be out in the fresh air and sun. I have a good tractor with a 54-inch deck for mowing and a nice hydraulic blade for plowing the snow.

There are about fifty trees on Bittersweet Farm, not including dozens growing over the stone wall on the west property line that runs along the border between Summit Township and Spring Arbor Township. Bittersweet is in Summit.

About twenty-five of the trees growing on Bittersweet Farm are walnuts; the rest are mostly maple and oak. The two acres of Bittersweet Farm form a rectangle, with the long end running north and south. It is high on the north and south ends and low in the middle, and the walnut grove grows low near the center of the property. The house and barn are in the southwest quarter of the rectangle.

The air is alive with birdsong, especially in the hour after dawn and the hour before sunset—the golden hours. Beginning at dusk, the fireflies begin to blink and hover over the lawns and fields. The way the land is laid over the earth creates an amphitheater effect: sounds carry beautifully. So when I play my harmonica on the porch at night or whistle or play the guitar, the sound is as lively as an old cathedral. On a good evening at dusk, the birdsong quiets and the owls begin to call. Barred owls call from the forest across the road south of the farm. It's a loud, haunting, beautiful sound.

If you have been paying attention, you know that the little farmhouse on Bittersweet was built with two porches. Hope rises early and brews coffee and goes out on the east-facing porch to read her Bible and have a time of quiet. She likes to call that porch the Sunrise Porch. Almost every evening, the three of us and whatever guests are visiting spend the last hour or so of daylight out in the south-facing porch, or the front porch. I like to call it the Evening Porch. Lois has splashed both porches with color and beauty using hanging pots of flowers.

A year ago was the summer of travel and preaching and camps and the summer of The Red Jeep Journey and The Red Jeep Journal. This summer is the summer of Bethel—just staying in town and serving my church. I have scheduled only one week of summer camp this year. I'm preaching and teaching and coaching and leading and encouraging and comforting and challenging and praying and counseling and getting to know the families of Bethel and their stories.

Bittersweet Farm
June 20, 2018

Chapter Twenty-Two

In a Cluster of Maples

We have passed through a trial, but our daughter and her children are still very much feeling the hurt of it and may do so all their lives. We know that as long as we are on this earth we will still battle the brokenness in our world, in our family, and in our own hearts. In our first year here we were visited with another great sadness. I wrote about that in August:

The family has quickly adopted Bittersweet Farm almost like a home-place. It is so clear to everyone that God was in it. Late in our first summer, that became clear to us when our daughter Hannah and her husband, Dale, made a cluster of maples east of the house a place especially sacred.

On Sunday our daughter Hannah and her husband Dale came to visit. They are traveling through the valley of the shadow of death, and they didn't want to do it alone.

They came over from their home in Grand Haven to visit. They brought their broken hearts with them. We stood in a very, very sad little circle by a cluster of trees on Bittersweet Farm and committed the remains of their precious little Lakelyn Dale to the earth.

Lois put a statue of a little girl over the spot, and with that gesture the ground there became holy ground—a sacred place. Wendell Berry once wrote:

"There are no un-sacred places;
there are only sacred places
and desecrated places."

For the most part I deeply agree with the statement, but this little spot at the foot of the shady cluster of maples became especially consecrated to us in that moment. In giving tiny Lakelyn Dale a place on the earth and in speaking her name, I could feel a measure of healing flow into each of our hearts. We held hands and prayed, and tears fell to the green earth.

Today they will celebrate their fifth anniversary. The day Hannah was married she danced, and I've never seen her so joyful. On Sunday she mourned, and I've never seen her so sad.

There is a time to weep and there is a time to laugh
There is a time to mourn and there is a time to dance

This is a season of weeping and mourning. There will be sunny days of laughter and dancing again…like the day we all see the little girl named Lakelyn, whom we never met but loved for a few weeks.

Bittersweet Farm
August 2018

CHAPTER TWENTY-THREE

A QUIET PLACE ON EARTH

Lord, Help Me Never to Lose the Wonder

I pull quietly away from Bittersweet Farm this morning
a few minutes after dawn.

I aim my car through a tunnel of trees
just west of the house.

Just beyond the trees I crest a hill.
A wide vista opens before me.

There, hanging in the western sky, is a full moon
silver in the blue sky over a vast field of green.

Across the sky flying southeast are a half-dozen beautiful
sandhill cranes crossing the sky just under the moon.

I breathe a prayer:
"Lord, help me never to lose the wonder of that."

Bittersweet Farm
August 29, 2018

A Quiet Place on the Earth

"Find me a place on the earth where a weary man can rest and listen for your voice in the turning seasons." —Fernando Ortega, "A Place on Earth"

Well, summer is all but over. It's the time of the turning of the seasons. The kids have returned to school. Now we can begin to recover from all the exhausting effort we put into taking it easy this summer.

In June, July, and August, most Michiganders go north. I have in my mind a picture of a big SUV pulling a trailer laden with toys and bikes and kayaks headed north to find a quiet place by the lake for a few days of rest. "It must be a lot of work to pull all that off," I think. In September we come back home and settle in and check the antifreeze, storm windows, and snow blower.

It's September in Michigan and hard to imagine a better time of the year to sit on the steps in the quiet morning or stroll in the waning evening, quiet before God. Saints and poets know there is something unusually stimulating about solitude and silence.

Jesus was often busy and surrounded with clamoring need, sickness and shame, brokenness and blindness, suffering and poverty, oppression and death. He often rose early and worked late preaching and healing and forgiving sinners and resisting religious perversion and casting out demons, but he also retreated to the wild and spent time with his Father in unhurried prayer. He taught his followers to do the same. He still does.

Mark wrote: "The apostles returned to Jesus and told him all that they had done and taught. And he said to them, 'Come away by yourselves to a desolate place and rest a while.' For many were coming and going, and they had no leisure even to eat. And they went away in the boat to a desolate place by themselves" (Mark 6:30-32, ESV).

Jesus, who retreated to the wild and taught his disciples to do the same, he is my King, he is my Lord, and he is my role model. I want to work hard, go about doing good, and rest well, as he did. I want time in the wild, hearing from God and breathing out praise, thanksgiving, confession, and sharing the desires of my heart with him. To do that, I'm going to take advantage of some time on the front steps watching the leaves blow down or the storm roll in.

I will not be distracted by reading, writing, projects, deadlines, or goals. I will not give in to the temptation to worry or fill my life with frenetic activity. I will be quiet. Walking, driving the countryside with the windows down in the evening, listening with heart and ears.

I commend this Christlike behavior to you. It's life-giving.

Jesus said: "Come to me, all you who are weary and burdened, and I will give you rest. Take my yoke upon you and learn from me, for I am gentle and humble in heart, and you will find rest for your souls. For my yoke is easy and my burden is light" (Matthew 11:28–29, NIV).

Bittersweet Farm
September 2018

CHAPTER TWENTY-FOUR

NODDING GOLDENROD AND AUTUMN WORRIES

It's a nice fall Saturday on Bittersweet Farm. It's been very warm and sunny, but last night a cold front came through — literally blew in. Temps dropped into the 40s overnight. First frost isn't due until early October, but that is only a few weeks away.

I rose early to pray with the Bethel elders as I do every Saturday. Lois and I did a couple of little projects together. She made granola. The house smelled like almonds, sunflower seeds, and cinnamon. I did a few small chores to help Lois and Hope and did some light car maintenance. College football murmurs in the background — never far from mind on a day like this.

I puttered around the carriage house a bit. Now I'm in my "reading chair" and Haz is currently curled up on the footstool. Hope is making dinner. Later I will again go over my message for tomorrow.

Goldenrod nods in the sunny breeze, and leaves are turning. The woods are blushing with color. First the yellows — elm and locust in September. The maples will flame orange and red in October, and then the oaks will linger brown and rust into November.

There are about thirty mature walnut trees on Bittersweet Farm. Every few minutes a walnut will fall from high in the trees and "thump" in the yard. People are busy taking care of business before the cold weather comes. Every night six or eight deer bed down in our back acre. Their coats are darkening for winter. I wonder how aware they are of the mayhem about to explode around them in November.

Among the good things about living in a state like Michigan are the mellow month of September; the crisp, colorful beauty of October; and the gray and brown month of November, ending in a weekend of thanksgiving. They create a three-month reminder to take care of business and keep your affairs in order at all times. This is good for your soul.

My thoughts and worries turn into prayers when I lie in bed on a cool autumn night beside my wife of almost forty years, under an extra blanket, wondering when I should cave in and let the furnace warm the old house. That's the way it should be.

Bittersweet Farm
September 22, 2018

Chapter Twenty-Five

Bad for My Writing, but Good for My Soul

It was one year ago today that we found Bittersweet Farm. We came across it while looking at another property. When I first saw it, I cried out in surprise, "Look, it's a John Sloane house!"

The place reminded me of the country houses painted by John Sloane, a favorite artist. Every year I would buy the John Sloane calendar. Every month I would stand quietly before it and turn the page on a new month and imagine I was standing in the picture or sitting on the porch or warm within, reading by a glowing light.

We immediately recognized the smiling providence of God that afternoon. It was the first of October, nearing the golden hour in the late afternoon. The sky was clear and shirtsleeves comfortable. We walked through the house and around the property, and before we left we had an agreement to buy the place. The owner, Charles Perlos, took the house off the market until we could sell Granville Cottage back in Riverview.

By mid-January, Granville Cottage sold, and that afternoon Bittersweet Farm was ours.

This afternoon I took a little drive in George the Red Jeep with the windows down, slow along a remote road a few miles east of here. I separated a doe from her fawn. The fawn ran along in the woods parallel to my Jeep until he could return to his mother.

Tonight I found more bittersweet growing in the fencerow that runs along the Spring Arbor-Summit Township line that is the western border of our property. Geese passed overhead in a perfect wedge formation. Crows called out over the corn. Walnuts thumped to the ground. Leaves danced along the ground ahead of the wind.

I got out my little John Deere and mowed, breathing in the fragrance of new-cut grass. You think when you mow. Tonight I thought about how many more times I will need to mow, when the leaves will come down, and when I should perform my annual maintenance and attach the snow plow. The experienced guys in the church will know. I will ask them.

Mowing, I watched the house. A little light shone from within. I was waiting for Hope to step out on the porch and call me in for supper. Lois was making one of our favorites tonight. I finished the lawn, put away the tractor, and came into the house. Supper was ready. The house smelled like apples and cinnamon.

Bittersweet Farm hasn't been good for my writing, but it has been good for my soul. I don't want to come inside until a half-hour after dark, and then I'm tired and my thinking isn't crisp, so I put my writing aside—but my soul is glad and my body is tired. I crawl into our high bed. It sits between the south-facing windows in our upstairs bedroom. When the moon is shining, the light falls into the room on either side of the bed. Some nights I put my arm around Lois. She rests her head on my chest. We lie together in quiet security and humble thankfulness, and we pray for the children and we thank God for Bethel and for Bittersweet Farm.

Bittersweet Farm
October 1, 2018

CHAPTER TWENTY-SIX

SATISFIED HEARTS

We've been sleeping with an extra cover on the bed for the last few weeks, but tonight the temperature is dipping into the 40s, so we turned on the furnace. Down in the basement the faithful appliance goes to work, and in a couple minutes a beautiful stream of warmth fills the room to just the perfect temperature and then falls quiet.

Last week I decided to test the furnace to be sure it was ready for the season. It wasn't. I called Keith Gillmore, who is as handy as they come and an expert at furnaces. He came over tonight for a good talk and noticed that a part that was supposed to be turning was not turning. He removed a few screws and discovered a dead bat was plugging the works.

We stood outside for a bit to talk about furnaces and restoring old cars and making cider. Keith grew up on a farm with an orchard, making cider. I asked him if he missed it this time of year. He said he didn't, but a smile comes to his face as he tells his cider-house stories. Something about it just seems right standing out in the cool of an October nightfall while the farmer back of Bittersweet Farm shaves the last remaining rows of corn off his place and pours the precious fruit of the earth into a waiting grain truck.

I love living in a place where deer and wild turkeys stroll around the back acre, geese and cranes soar overhead, bittersweet grows in the rocky fencerow, and bats and other critters flit and steal about in the darkness. The windows are closed to the night air tonight, but my walk will be bracing in the morning.

The trees bending over the road are beginning to turn orange and yellow. When the sun's rays fall on them, they irradiate their color. Something in the beauty of it leaps into our soul.

When I drive through a tunnel of October-tinted trees, it is a worship experience without fail. My heart rises up in grateful praise. The Great Artist of the Universe did not have to paint with such vivid and captivating colors, but he did. He did it as a witness to his goodness to draw your soul upward to him.

Jesus himself is the Great Creator, and only he can satisfy your heart. He alone should have your heart.

On one of the Apostle Paul's church-planting missions, he visited Lystra. God allowed Paul and Barnabas to heal a man who had not been able to walk from birth. When the people of Lystra saw this, they tried to worship Paul and Barnabas. The men quickly reminded them that only God, who made the heaven and the earth and all that is in them, was worthy of worship and able to satisfy the deepest longings of their souls.

"Yet he did not leave himself without witness, for he did good by giving you rains from heaven and fruitful seasons, satisfying your hearts with food and gladness" (Acts 14:17, ESV).

There is something to think about when you are lying in your bed on a cool October night and you hear the furnace kick on.

Bittersweet Farm
October 8, 2018

CHAPTER TWENTY-SEVEN

HOME BEFORE DARK

I returned from church this afternoon in time to take a long walk afield. It was in the high 50s and sunny. A walk on a Michigan autumn evening is a sacramental act. The sky is October blue, the trees brushed with color. The corn is dry and brown, but it's been rainy and we are still ahead of the first frost, so the grass is green and lush.

After my walk, I sat out on the porch and read, draining the very last drop for the bottom of the cup of this sweet Lord's Day. Finally the sunlight dropped into the trees. The evening grew chill. I stepped down into the leaf-strewn yard and looked west one more time to where the sun had dropped behind the trees, just in time to see a perfect V-shaped flock of geese cross the sky over the farm, honking their way south and west over the line of trees.

Your Default Home Setting
Last week I received permission from the woman who owns the land north and east of Bittersweet Farm to freely walk her property. The generous gesture moved me to tears. It is a large tract of land that includes farm fields, wetland, and woods. So I set off exploring on a brisk October Friday.

When I dress for work, Hazard ignores me, but he can tell when I'm dressing for a walk and he follows me around the house while I'm getting ready as if to say: "Take me too. Take me too." I took him along and walked due north of Bittersweet Farm along the rocky, overgrown fencerow. We had covered about a mile going north into the field behind that, skirting the east side of a low spot and woods. So two long fields run end to end north of us, and woods are north of that. Beyond that, further north, is the Falling Waters Trail. Just south of the woods, I let Hazard off his lead. He would run ahead and I would call him back before he got too far.

We repeated this a half-dozen times, and then I got distracted by a huge deer rub and about twenty sandhill cranes fishing and sunning in the pond at the south edge of the woods. I surprised them and they all rose into the air flapping their huge wings and calling out with their loud rattle-like call. They flew over the trees and east out of sight. By the time I climbed back to the high ground, little Hazard was nowhere in sight. I called to him. He didn't come.

I called Lois and told her that Hazard was lost. We prayed we could find him before Hope got off work. I turned and started the long walk back to the house. Along the way I called for Hazard. I worried that he might have strayed onto the property west of us, where we don't have the right to walk. It took me a half-hour or more to get back to the line of trees that separate the two fields north of the house.

When I walked along the north side of the thicket, I could hear Hazard barking. A smile came to my face when I realized that when he could not find me, he beat it straight for home. No one was there, but he was standing on the porch barking for someone to let him in.

He has a powerful instinct for home.

This week at Bethel I started a series of messages about Jonah, the prophet who, when he received his assignment, thought he could flee from the presence of God. I told the people this: There are three things I want to tell you about fleeing from the presence of God.

First, it is natural to flee from God because of our sin.

Second, it is impossible to flee from the presence of God because of his power.

Third, it is foolish to flee from the presence of God because of his mercy and love.

The rest of the afternoon I sat in my chair and did some reading. Little Haz curled up on the ottoman at my feet, safe, secure, and well-fed. Take a lesson from Ol' Haz: train your soul to run for God whenever you are lost or lonely or burdened with guilt or shame.

Bittersweet Farm
October 15, 2018

Home Before Dark
The other evening I was clearing away a few leaves and Lois was puttering around the outside of the house. It was a lingering fall evening—the kind that gives you the sense that they are short and few and will soon be gone. She lit

some candles on the porch and in the house. My heart was glad for her. We are different in many ways, but the longer we live together (almost forty years now), the more I see that the things we agree on are powerful.

—We both deeply love Jesus and want to build our lives on the truth of the Bible.

—We both are devoted to our children and grandchildren—that they would know and love the Lord.

—We love our home, Bittersweet Farm... and know it was a special gift of God to us.

—We are deeply thankful for Bethel Church and know it, too, was a special grace from God to us.

—We are both childlike, intuitive, creative types...

—We don't worry—we are not overly "responsible." That keeps us young and light on our feet.

But there are a couple things more that we agree on that are as small as they are sweet.

We like to light small lights to drive out the darkness and create and atmosphere. That is one reason we like to say, "On Bittersweet Farm, every day is a beautiful day and the little light in the kitchen is always on." We believe in the little light in the kitchen...

And another is like unto it...We don't have to, but we like to get home before dark. We are often out late, of course, because of the ministry or visiting family, but on an evening when we go out for a drive or for coffee, or when we go to Horton's for ice cream, we like to time our trip so that we pull back into Bittersweet farm before dark. In the dusk, the little light burning within welcomes us home...Going around lighting up dark places and seeing people home before dark...that is what we are about.

And may all the children be home before dark.

Bittersweet Farm
October 26, 2018

CHAPTER TWENTY-EIGHT

A ROCK IN THE WOODS

November on Bittersweet Farm. It's our first November on Bittersweet Farm. The trees are almost bare of leaves. I've spent some time mowing and mulching and blowing them into the fields and woods.

Shepherd's Pie. Lois surprised me with a wonderful shepherd's pie for my birthday on Saturday. Hannah and Dale came with Mom and Dad. There was chocolate cake with chocolate frosting after dinner. (There was also chocolate cake with chocolate frosting for my birthday party at the church on Thursday and chocolate cake with chocolate frosting for the men's prayer breakfast on Saturday.)

Bathed in Prayer. A new Jan Karon book came to the house on the first day of its publication. It is called *Bathed in Prayer, Father Tim's Prayers, Sermons, and Reflections from the Mitford Series*. It has a delightful red hardcover with a nice ribbon marker.

Under the Unpredictable Plant, Jonah and Bethel. Eugene Peterson went to be with the Lord. He had written a book on Jonah for pastors called *Under the*

Unpredictable Plant. I'm reading it to think of him and to prepare my heart for the Jonah series. The series has been well received. Bethel is growing. Today it seemed full, though we could fit about a hundred more in if people moved to the middle and we filled the balcony. Bethel is a singing church. There was love and energy in the building today. We celebrated communion. I reminded the people that communion commemorates our union with Christ, which empowers our communion with each other.

Autumn Visitors. Friday night I worked hard to clear the leaves from the yard. When I backed Grenfell out in the dark morning on the way to the men's prayer breakfast, no one was coming, so I paused to take a good long look at my work. It always pleases me to watch the house and imagine people sleeping securely within, light glowing from the kitchen. I breathe a prayer and drive away. When I looked up to start down the road, there, on the south side of the road, standing and looking at me, waiting for me to pass, was a large buck. After I drove away, he quietly crossed the road.

Late Saturday night I was standing in the yard at dusk and heard coyotes howling somewhere in the far north field or in the woods beyond.

In the last week or so I have often stood in the yard toward evening and watched geese migrate overhead, usually going southwest for some reason. I never tire of watching them fly over and hearing their calls.

A Rock in the Woods
I preached two funerals this weekend. Both were for 90-year-old long-time Bethel women. One of them had a habit

for years of taking walks in the woods. She had a large rock deep in the woods. She used the rock as a place to pray.

I have a couple rocks where I can sit and rest, or think or pray. They are in the hedgerows, which in this region are filled with beautiful stones.

It's important to have quiet, private places to think and pray and retreat from noise and enjoy solitude. These things are good for our souls. I love the warm cabin of Grenfell (my Toyota Camry) in the winter or fall or the warm cabin of George the Red Jeep. I have had many sweet, quiet hours with the Lord, driving through the night praying or worshipping with the light from the instrument panels reflecting on my face.

My heart remembers and never will forget driving to my speaking engagements in George the Red Jeep or Grenfell or driving away with the faces of the people in my memory.

Bittersweet Farm
November 5, 2018

CHAPTER TWENTY-NINE

THEY MUST HAVE PRAYED FOR US

Around the holidays, especially, the family comes to visit Bittersweet Farm. All too soon they have to leave and we are standing in the drive holding back tears and watching them drive away. Every day they are on our hearts, and especially at night when we lie in bed, they are in our prayers. After our first Thanksgiving on Bittersweet Farm, I put down my thoughts:

They Must Have Prayed for Us
Thanksgiving ended, and a little at a time the children took the grandchildren, strapped them in their little car seats, and drove away. As is our custom, we stand and wave until they disappear over the hill to the west, and then we walk back into the house with a lump in our throats.

We pick up the little things they left lying around, and everything reminds us of them, what they said, and the little people they are becoming. We tidy the house and put things back in order...

And we pray.

We pray that these dark and evil times will not crush the life out of them. We pray that they will have the endurance to stand against the strong tide of evil that pushes against them. We pray that the children will be safe and well, that they will know God intimately and love him deeply.

We pray that they will turn their back on the empty promises the world makes and build their lives on the promises of the Word of God.

We remind ourselves that we are not the only generation, not the only people, who have had to keep the fire of our faith alive while cold winds of cynicism and skepticism, immorality and infidelity threaten to blow it out.

We climb the stairs to bed and we talk and our hearts breathe out prayer to God for their lives and their precious souls. More and more, the world around them is filled with people living in open rebellion toward God or in dark ignorance of God.

We pray that they will flourish spiritually, a remnant of faithfulness, a faithful minority in whom the sweet Holy Spirit of God dwells.

We pray that they will be holy and happy and healthy, filled with all the fullness of God and strengthened with might by his power in their inner person.

We pray that they will be among those of whom Paul wrote to the Ephesians there would be "glory in the church through all generations."

We pray and plead with God to keep growing us into the example they need of people living in joyful and complete dependence upon God.

We pray and confess our great weakness, our poor examples, our failures and sins and selfishness—all of the ugly things in us that might have distracted them from the beauty of Jesus.

Then we drift off to sleep and wake up in the night and their faces come before us. We remember the things we said to them. We remember the words they said to us. We know in the stillness of the night that You alone are our only hope and help. You alone are their only hope and help.

I wonder if my grandparents, who all came to know and love the Lord in midlife, felt the same way about us when we drove away from a long holiday weekend together. Then I remember their sober faces and their eyes searching our eyes for understanding. I remember their affirmations of love, the preparations they made, the tender warnings they gave. When I think of it I remember their gentle warnings and their worn Bibles, and I remember their habits of faith and faithfulness. I remember their practical gifts. I remember their humble homes. I remember the little circles of prayer when we parted and their tearful eyes.

And then I know that when we drove out of sight they must have gone to their rooms and they must have lain in their beds and their hearts must have ached with tenderness and they must have prayed for us. They must have remembered the things I said. They would have noticed how quickly I had grown since last I saw them. They must have wanted to open my little heart and take the love of God they had found and put it into mine…I'm sure they worried. It was the sixties. The world was becoming a scary place to raise kids.

They prayed. I'm sure of it. Sure of it. And they are with the Lord now and they have been for years. But I have built my life on the promises of God. I have placed my hope in the God of my fathers and the God of my mothers. Those people who stood waving goodbye walked back into the house fighting back tears, lay in their beds, and prayed. Carried their Bibles to church and sang and prayed and listened to the preaching of God's Word and hoped for grandchildren who would follow Jesus.

Bittersweet Farm
November 25, 2018

CHAPTER THIRTY

RUSTLING WITH RUMORS

Our son Daniel was married in Gallup, New Mexico. It seemed like a foreign country to us. It was beautiful, stark, strange, and wonderful all at once. The wedding was a joyful occasion, and when it was over the couple left on their honeymoon and the siblings all went home via a side trip to Colorado. Lois and I, Hope, our daughter Holly, and her husband, Jesse, stayed behind.

We found a good church and attended services there on the Lord's Day. After lunch we got some much-needed sleep. In the evening we went to a little restaurant downtown, not so much to eat as to have a place to be together. Sometimes it's hard to arrange a good place in public for conversation, but the Lord smiled upon us that night.

The sun was out as it usually is in that part of the world. There was dancing in the town square. It was peaceful. The food was good; then we drifted into easy conversation.

I had been thinking about a book of stories that was on my heart. Stories of God's unusual province. Times when God guided or provided or warned us in an unusual way. Whenever I got with people and time would allow, I would ask them a question like this: "Do you remember a time when you feel God spoke to you or a time of unusual circumstances that could only have been arranged by God?"

Jesse told me a story about how God confirmed his decision to go as a missionary for four years to Tanzania. We drifted into easy and meaningful conversation about the Lord's direction, the Lord's work, the Lord's provision. How one obedience leads to another.

We talked about how Holly grew to admire him while reading the blog of his missionary work in Tanzania and how that ultimately drew them together from opposite sides of the country.

We lingered over our soft drinks and even now, years later, I think on that conversation with fondness because it was a conversation about things that deeply matter—ultimate things...

A Circle of Christian Friends by a Good Fire
I was reading of the conversion of C. S. Lewis the other day and came across this passage from a letter he wrote to one of his students, capped with a lyrical line that I love...In it he was talking about conversations about things that are good turning into conversations about things that are ultimate...

"We meet on Friday evenings in my rooms," Lewis says, "theoretically to talk about literature, *but in fact nearly always to talk about something better.* What I owe to them is incalculable. Dyson and Tolkien were immediate human causes of my own conversion. Is any pleasure on earth as great as a circle of Christian friends by a good fire?"

The fire helps. The food helps. Literature is good. Sports are good. Essential oils are good. Football is good. Child training is good. Landscaping is good. These are good things, but they are not ultimate things.

That is why we often have a sense of longings unfulfilled. We are not fully satisfied now, even as believers, but as C. S. Lewis said in his address captured in *The Weight of Glory*, we are not satisfied now, *"…but all the pages of the New Testament rustle with the rumors that it will not always be so…."* Later he says, *"One day—one day the door upon which we have been knocking all our lives will open at last…."*

We will then experience full and ultimate joy, fulfillment, satisfaction in the presence of God…

Things that are good but not ultimate are meant to arouse a longing for things that are eternal and ultimate.

Timothy Keller has written, "Idolatry is when good things become ultimate things." When that happens, there will be an intense level of emptiness. All the world is bittersweet and it will be until all things become new, but if we don't understand that, we will never experience the sweetness of contemplation and conversation about ultimate things…

And people. This is what Jesus meant for his church to be.

Bittersweet Farm
January 6, 2019

WINTER MERCIES

The sacrament of a south-facing window.

A half-moon high in the starry sky
shining down though bare tree branches.

A doe silent in the tree line alternately eating
and lifting her head to watch me.

The breath of my prayers hanging silver on the night air.

These are winter mercies...
For which my heart is deeply thankful.

Bittersweet Farm
January 2019

PART THREE:

THE CHARLES PERLOS STORY

Charles Perlos was the man who sold us Bittersweet Farm. The day we met, we both knew that God had put us together. I knew that God had sent us along the road where he lived. I will always cherish the fact that we "happened" on the place by the direction of God, like finding a patch of bittersweet growing in a fencerow on an autumn afternoon. When I drove away, I told Lois that I knew God had sent me into his life. Charles told his daughter Lindy that he knew it was no accident that I came along. God was doing something.

He didn't say much about it at the time, but he was a sick man. He didn't complain, but he traveled every week to Houston for treatments for cancer. He was quietly fighting hard for his life.

When Charles and I talked, the conversation always seemed to toggle back and forth between Bittersweet Farm and the things of the Lord. We were within about a month of each other in age, but our worlds had been different. Our political loyalties did not line up perfectly. Our backgrounds were different. His people had money and were well connected. We were simple people with little money or social connections. Our best conversations were about things that were ultimate, and the closer Charles got to going to meet the Lord, the more of those conversations we had.

If you have walked with the Lord for a while, you get a sense when God is doing something. This I knew. God was doing something when he sent us down that road and into the life of Charles Perlos.

CHAPTER THIRTY-ONE

Saturday Morning Prayer Meetings

At Bethel we have a prayer meeting for the elders every Saturday morning. Once a month we invite all the men of the church to join us, and we gather around round tables for coffee and breakfast and prayer.

In the first meeting of the elders, they had expressed their concern over what they perceived as a weakness in the church—a lack of evangelism. They said they were looking to me for leadership on how to approach evangelism. Immediately a simple strategy sprang to mind. I'd spent the last number of years developing a simple plan to help people in local churches anywhere, of any size, make disciples. I explained it to the men, and they immediately adopted it.

That morning I said: "Men, let's not talk about this or explain it to the church. Let's just begin to do it ourselves and pray for fruit. When God gives us stories to tell, we will tell them."

The strategy was simple and it began with prayer. Each of us would have a list of people who did not know the Lord for whom we would pray regularly—perhaps daily. And our prayer would be: "Lord, how do you want me to love them?"

At the time I was still commuting from the Riverview 75 miles every day. The only person in Jackson that I knew who was not involved at Bethel was my friend Charles Perlos, from whom we hoped to buy the house.

The day I met Charles, I was convinced that God had sent me down that road to help him. I was not sure that we would ever get to buy the little farm, but I had a strong sense that I would have ongoing ministry in his life.

The day he showed us the house, I picked up on the fact that he was a person with regard for belief.

After talking for some time I said, "You are a man of faith, aren't you?"

"I am," he answered readily.

So I began to pray every day for Charles Perlos to be saved. I began to ask God, "How can I love him?"

I would have lunch with him from time to time and develop a friendship with him and show interest in his life. Later it came to my heart to give him a copy of my book. One day I drove to the farm and left a copy on the back porch.

Not long after that, I called to let him know that we were showing the house and anticipating some offers. I didn't want to bother him, but I wanted to keep my foot in the door so that he would not sell the place to someone else before we were able to sell our home.

On the phone that day he said something every writer longs to hear: "I read your book. It was very good. I enjoyed it. You are a good author."

He went on to describe some of the stories in the book and ended with "I can see now why you are so interested in the house. I think you will really like it here."

I continued to pray. I considered Charles not just a man of faith in God, but a God-fearer, like Cornelius, a Roman centurion whose story is in the Book of Acts. Cornelius prayed, and he gave gifts, but he did not yet fully understand salvation. The Lord sent Peter to him to make salvation plain. As soon as Cornelius understood the way to God, he became a believer. I saw Charles as a God-fearer like Cornelius.

I considered him a man who did not yet fully understand salvation by grace through faith in Christ alone, but a man who was spiritually open, on his way to fully understanding Jesus and embracing him as his Savior.

Once we got moved to the area, I texted Charles and invited him to Bethel. He visited Bethel and I introduced him to the people. His daughter Lindy, his twin brother Mark, and his sister Pam attended that day. The people of Bethel thanked him for what he did to help us get Bittersweet Farm. He stood when I introduced him to the people. He seemed happy. I was glad to have him at Bethel.

Shortly after that, I texted Charles and asked him to go to lunch. I was sure he was ready to receive Christ as his Savior, but I was in for a surprise. I had misunderstood where he was in his spiritual journey.

CHAPTER THIRTY-TWO

HE'S MY BROTHER

It was a sunny day when we met for lunch. We talked about the farm and his treatments for cancer. He told me about his regular trips to Houston for treatments.

When lunch was done, I said: "Charles, I want to ask you a question. You are my friend. You showed a great kindness to our family that I will never forget. I want to be sure that you understand the way of eternal life clearly. Do you mind if I ask you a question?"

"No, not at all," he said, as he looked me in the eyes.

"I have an old friend who used to ask this question. I have always thought it was helpful. Here it is…"

I said, "Charles, do you think eternal life or heaven is a free gift, or is it something you have to earn?"

"Well," he said, "it is definitely something that had to be earned, because Jesus Christ had to die on the cross for us, but if we believe we receive eternal life as a free gift, that is what I believe. Is that what you believe?"

"Charles that is exactly what I believe. How did you learn that?"

"Well I've studied this on my own and I watch Billy Graham and David Jeremiah on television."

We walked to the car. "Charles, I have a gift I want you to have. It's a Bible in a very readable translation. I think you will like it."

Standing there by our cars he smiled and reached out and took it and said: "Thank you very much. Let me show you my favorite passage." He turned to Isaiah 41:10.

"I love this verse," he said, pointing to the passage and quoting it from memory: "So do not fear, for I am with you; do not be dismayed, for I am your God. I will strengthen you and help you; I will uphold you with my righteous right hand."

I drove away with a smile in my heart that day. All this time I was praying and planning to lead Charles to Christ. He was already my brother.

One Saturday night I was preparing my message when I stumbled on Isaiah 40:31. I texted Charles and told him that I was going to use his favorite verse in my sermon in the morning. He texted back immediately and said: "That is odd. I was listening to David Jeremiah and he just quoted that before you texted me. I will see you in the morning."

The next day Charles joined us at Bethel for worship. After church he told me: "Ken, I was looking around while you were preaching. The people were listening to every word. Man, they are really with you. I can see you belonged here."

CHAPTER THIRTY-THREE

CHRISTMAS ON BITTERSWEET FARM

At Christmastime we had a full house. As a result, we had a failure of our septic system. I remembered talking with Charlies Perlos about the septic system during our last meeting for lunch. I gave him a call with my questions. As always, he was especially candid and helpful.

The day after Christmas was a beautiful day in the low 50s, and I was sitting outside talking to him. About to hang up I said, "So how are you doing?"

"Not well," he said. "I've called hospice in. I'm not sure how long I have to live."

My heart was broken. "Can I come and see you?"

"I'd like that," he said.

I hung up the phone and wept. I sat in the yard for a while and thought about how God had so unmistakably led us together. My heart was heavy. I thought, "I wish I could baptize him."

Later that afternoon I drove over to see him. He was glad to see me. He was not well. Our conversations always seemed to center around two things: the farm I called Bittersweet and the things of the Lord. Often they ran together because they really were the same thing.

I didn't bring up baptism. I knew he had been sprinkled as a baby. I didn't want to offend him, but I deeply believe that believer's baptism is the first step of following Jesus, his first command after "repent and believe."

Suddenly Charles said, as if reading my mind, "I want to get baptized."

"That's wonderful, Charles," I said. "You know you do not have to be baptized to be saved…" He cut me off.

"I know. I know that," he said. "This is just something I know I should do. I want to be baptized."

"Charles, I love you. I'll do anything to help you. Our baptistery at Bethel is up a long flight of stairs. Maybe I can find another baptistery and we can meet there so you won't have to climb the stairs," I said.

We talked for a bit about that and about some other things, and then I said: "Well, the ball is in your court on the baptism. Let me know if there is anything I can do to help you."

The next time I visited Charles, he was burdened about preparing for death.

At one point he answered a question with this quip: "I'm not sure. This is the first time I've died. I've never done this before." Then he chuckled at his own joke.

"I want to be baptized."

"Charles," I said, "I could baptize you in the swimming pool up at Vista Grand Villa."

"No. I want to be baptized at Bethel."

"There is a full flight of steps there. I don't know if you could make that climb."

"I want to try."

It was a Thursday, just a few minutes before the secretary would leave for the weekend. I called Linda at the church and said: "Linda, I'm here with Charles Perlos. He wants to be baptized. Can you have Lindy fill the baptistery for Sunday? We will baptize him first thing in the service."

That night I told the people at the Advisory Council meeting about Charles's desire to be baptized at Bethel Church. They were eager to help. Four men volunteered to get him up the stairs.

The next Saturday I visited Charles. We talked about the things of the Lord. We talked about heaven. As always, we talked about Bittersweet Farm, the dark sadness that had sent us away from where we used to live, and the sweet goodness of God that had sent us down the road past Bittersweet Farm and into his life that golden October evening.

I walked him though the details of his baptism. We prayed. I said, "See you in the morning."

With all my heart I believe that when a person decides to walk with the Lord all the fury of hell rises up against him and all the forces of heaven are at his aid. It is spiritual warfare. I've noticed over the years that getting to the baptistery, that first act of obedience after repentance and faith, is a step that many do not take because there are dark forces opposing them.

CHAPTER THIRTY-FOUR

THE BAPTISM OF CHARLES PERLOS

The baptistery was full and warm, and all the preparations were made. I was in my study on Sunday morning and praying that nothing would prevent Charles from obeying the Lord in the testimony of baptism.

Charles was to arrive an hour ahead of the service to prepare. He was very, very sick and frail. It was a bitterly cold winter morning. I knew that it was likely he would not be there. I prayed, content to know that whether he was baptized or not, his faith was in Christ.

One of the men stepped into my study and said, "Pastor he's here, and he's going up the stairs on his own."

When the service opened that morning, the pre-service announcements were displayed on a video screen. The announcements included a countdown timer. When it was time for the service to begin, the screen went up and I was standing there in the baptistery to tell the story of Charles Perlos and Bittersweet Farm.

Charles had written out a personal testimony. This is what it said:

When my education was done and I was deep into marriage and fathering, I realized that there was more to life than ME.

There was more to life than fast cars, big homes, riches.

I began to see that I was here for a reason. I began to understand my purpose.

I wanted to teach my girls what they would need to survive in this life.

I wanted to help people who were poor, oppressed, guilty, injured, and those who were wrongfully accused.

(Ironically, I ended up being one of those people—not through the legal system, but God sent me to Charles's door to help him, and he arranged to have Charles there to help me.)

I realized that for some of the oppressed and guilty and injured—their fate and their freedom was in my hands, and I began to realize I could not do that alone. I would need God's help.

Now at 60, again, I am aware that I have sinned! I am a sinner in need of grace and forgiveness.

I said to the Lord: "Forgive me and come into my heart. I believe in you (like the guilty man dying beside Jesus on the cross…don't forget me…remember me when you come to your kingdom…").

I renounce Satan.

When I was done reading his testimony, the men helped him down into the baptismal pool.

"Charles Perlos," I said, "have you placed your faith and trust in Christ alone for your salvation?"

Clearly, he said, "Yes, I have."

"Charles Perlos, upon your profession of faith in Jesus Christ as your Lord and Savior, and in obedience to his command, I baptize you in the name of the Father, and of the Son, and of the Holy Spirit."

I lowered Charles into the water and raised him up, and he burst into a joyful smile. The congregation at Bethel began to clap and cheer; together, they all stood to their feet in an ovation of praise to God for what he had done.

CHAPTER THIRTY-FIVE

A PLACE PREPARED
FOR US

A couple weeks later, on a bitterly cold winter night, Charles's family called to tell me that he had moved to a hospice facility. It was dark and bitter, bitter cold outside. I bundled up and made my way to the facility. I parked as close as I could and hurried against the brutal cold to his room. He was surrounded by loving family members.

When I came into the room, he had been unresponsive all day. I took his hand and said, "Charles, it's Ken Pierpont."

He immediately opened his eyes and a smile crossed his face. His family said, "That is the most he has responded to anything all day."

They slipped out so I could talk with him alone. I talked to him for a bit, read him some Scripture, prayed.

"Charles," I said, "thank you so much for your kindness to me and to our family. Thanks for being my friend when I needed one. Thanks for helping me when I was falsely accused. I want you to know that God's holy angels are about to take you to be with the Lord. He loves you. You are his child. I love you too, and I will always be grateful for what you did. We will never forget you."

In the morning, first thing, I sat with him and his daughter Lindy for about an hour, read Scripture, prayed, and thanked him again for his kindness to us. Lindy said, "The day you first visited, after you left, Dad said, 'That was not an accident. That was meant to be.' "

It was. God sent us mercifully down the road that autumn afternoon. God moved Charles to renovate the house and to save it for us and to wait until we were able to buy it. He held our $1,000 down payment check until closing. He saved the house for us based on a handshake. He kept his word to us.

When I left his side on the day he slipped into the presence of Jesus, I reached out and touched his shoulder and said: "Goodbye, my friend. I will see you soon."

On an earlier visit, Charles had given us a large album of pictures of the renovation of our home. It's an amazing photo journal of the extensive restoration. Lois, Hope, and I live in a home that was prepared for us by Charles Perlos. As I walked away, I realized in my heart that when I next see Charles, we will both be enjoying the home the Jesus prepared for us. And I will have stories to tell him about the place we call Bittersweet Farm.

On Tuesday afternoon I will preach his funeral. I am only a month and a few days older than he was. He was my friend, and I will always thank God for him.

Bittersweet Farm
February 4, 2019

CHAPTER THIRTY-SIX

GOODBYE, FRIEND

Charles was fighting cancer the whole time I knew him. He didn't seem to want to talk about it. He fought it hard, but he also thoughtfully arranged the details of his life so that if he died it would not bring unnecessary hardship to his daughters. He was continually thinking of them.

He sold the farm because the master bedroom and bath were upstairs and he needed to have a place on one level. When I visited him in the weeks before his death, he asked me if I would preach his funeral. I agreed. Before Charles died, he told me he wanted the funeral in a downtown church at a time of day when it would be convenient for his friends and colleagues in the courthouse and downtown businesses to attend. He wanted his funeral to be held in a place familiar to his daughters. He was thinking of others.

On the day of his funeral, the church was full. The crowd filled every seat and spilled into the overflow. I didn't really preach. I simply told his story. That was all I needed to do.

Dennis Conant, one of our elders and a friend to Charles for many years, was there. He said to me, "Pastor, I love how you gave the gospel so clearly without preaching."

 It was true. The story was so powerful and the gospel embedded in it so sweetly that all I had to do was tell the story. The large downtown church was silent as they listened to the remarkable, bittersweet story.

After the service at the church, I followed the hearse to the cemetery and joined his family, dropping roses onto his casket.

CHAPTER THIRTY-SEVEN

HOME THE
BITTERSWEET WAY

After the graveside service, I took the back roads home by way of the Jackson County countryside. It was a beautiful winter day. I drove in silence. Warmth filled the car, though snow covered the fields and lingered in the tree branches.

Charles and I shared a love for this part of the country. We both loved nature and birds and the countryside. We often talked about sitting out on the porch. He knew I was a writer, and he had some stories to tell me.

Once he told me how when he was a boy, his father, who was a judge in Jackson County, would take him to their country property on weekends. His mother would make him a cheese sandwich. His dad and brothers would stop at a little country store out this way for soda from the old machine where the glass bottles sat in cold water and you would fish your bottle out in the little maze. They would fish

and tramp around until dark and then make their way back
to town. He'd loved this area since he was a child.

"Ken, you write. I have stories I can tell you about that
place and the history of the area. You know there was an
unsolved murder a little over a mile across country out on
Horton Road, don't you?" he once told me.

"It happened in 1823. They are all buried behind that little
church on the corner of Reynolds and Horton Roads. No
one knows to this day who killed them...the whole family
was killed, and they never found the murderer. The place
was just off the railroad track that used to run through here
on the way to Chicago. The train would stop there. People
wanted to see the place where the murder happened. It is
still unsolved."

I wondered what else he had to say about the countryside
around Bittersweet Farm, but I would never know.

With sadness I realized that we would never have those
conversations. I would not have another conversation with
him this side of heaven. In the quietness of my thoughts,
driving through the countryside, I remembered back to our
last conversation before he was taken to hospice. It was at
his home.

You Need to Relax. Have Faith.
When I arrived at his home that day, he was a little
troubled. It seemed to me that he was trying to tie up loose
ends—to get his personal affairs in order, and something
was bothering him.

I said: "Charles, let me ask you a question. Are you depending on your righteousness or the righteousness of Christ?"

He didn't answer right away...

I said: "Let me ask you another way. Imagine at the gate of heaven you were asked, 'Should I let you in here based on your righteousness, your goodness, or should I let you in based on the goodness and the righteousness of Christ?' "

"Well, Christ's righteousness," he said, but his answer was halting. Then something very powerful hit me.

After we had agreed that he would sell us the home we call Bittersweet Farm, Charles drafted papers. He was an attorney. He ordered inspections. He gave us until December to sell our house with a clause that allowed us, by mutual agreement, to extend the terms to the first of January.

When I met Charles I was immediately convinced that God had sent us down that particular road on that October day. When we drove away, we knew we wanted to buy that house, but we were not at all sure that would ever happen. I was deeply convinced, based on our conversation that day, that God had sent me into Charles Perlos's life. I told Lois as we drove away, "I don't know if we will ever get to live there, but I do believe God sent me to meet Charles."

It took a while for us to get our house prepared to go on the market. We were unsure about the details and inexperienced in selling a home. We had inspections and repairs to make. I was commuting out to Jackson every day from the Detroit Downriver, leaving before light and arriving home tired after dark. We were not at all sure things were going to work out, but we were praying continually that they would.

Charles must have sensed my concerns. When I talked to him during that time, he would say: "Relax. This will all work out. You need to have faith."

Finally, our house in the Downriver sold, and the day after the money from the sale hit our bank, we arranged to meet Charles at the title company in Jackson to close on the farm. At the closing, we sat across the table from each other. I kept hoping that some last-minute hitch would not crush our dream to buy the place.

We took care of all the paperwork, and the deal was complete. Bittersweet Farm was ours. Lois and I were so deeply thankful to God for Bethel, for Charles, for Bittersweet Farm; we shed tears of thankfulness for what God had done. God had taken something so evil, so unjust, and turned it into something so good, so beautiful. He had taken something so bitter and turned it into something so sweet.

I looked across the table at Charles, and with tears pooling in my eyes, I said: "Charles, we don't know how to thank you. We love the place so much. We are so grateful to you for restoring the house so beautifully and for being willing to sell it to us. Thank you for taking it off the market and waiting until our house sold."

His eyes also filled with tears, and he smiled and said as he often had said before: "I told you to relax, didn't I? I told you; you need to have faith."

"Charles, I hope we have not seen the last of you. I would very much like to be friends. Maybe we can meet for lunch from time to time at Knights. I want to be your friend. I'd like you to stop out by the house come spring. We can sit on the porch and you can tell me all the stories you know about the place and the history and the area."

"That sounds good," he said. "We will do that."

We shook hands and I thanked him and we drove away to see our new home. We owned Bittersweet Farm. God had given it to us.

Now, sitting in his home, having what I did not know would be my last conversation with him, it came to me how I could help him understand fully what Christ had done for him, how I could help him lean into the righteousness of Christ.

"Charles, do you remember that autumn day when you stood on the back porch and I stood on the steps and I told you I would give you your asking price and you promised to sell the place to us?"

"I do."

"Charles, I would call you, and you would tell me, 'Ken, you need to relax. Trust me.' "

"I remember that. The problem was you didn't know me. You didn't know that I was a man who does what he says, who keeps his word."

"Don't you see, Charles? That is what Jesus is saying to you right now: 'Charles, you need to trust me. I promised. I will do what I said. I promise that if you believe in me I will give you eternal life. Now you just need to trust me.' "

Suddenly it was like a light swept across his countenance, and he smiled and said: "Oh, that's good. I see. You are right. That's good."

We talked for a while about the farm and about his family. We talked about his parents and his sister and his brothers. We talked about his wife and about his daughters. As always, we talked a little more about the farm.

I've noticed something profound in forty years of pastoral work. Trouble comes into every life in this sin-cursed world. No one escapes it, but people are different in the way they respond to trouble. When trouble comes, some people turn away from God, they walk away from God; they may even run from God. Others turn to God when trouble comes. They have grace to run to God and not away. It's clear to see. In trouble, Charles turned to God. He appreciated prayer. He was moved when people promised to pray for him. He was eager to read the Scriptures. He loved Bible preaching and teaching and sought it out.

His daughter told me that one morning she came out to the kitchen and noticed that he had been sitting at the island and reading his Bible, making marks in it with a highlighter. After he left for work, she picked up his Bible and paged through it. In many different places in his Bible he had highlighted favorite passages.

Whenever we talked, he was especially hungry for truth from the Bible. That day when I visited, it was bitter cold outside. A nice fire in a little gas stove warmed the room, and there, by the warmth of the fire, the conversation centered on things that are eternal and ultimate. We prayed. He thanked me.

"This has been good," he said. "This has been so helpful. Thank you. I feel much better."

I turned before I left and said, "I love you, Charles."

When I put on my shoes and walked to the car over the pine cones in the snow in the front yard, my heart was glad, glad to know that my friend had rooted his hope in Christ, and my heart was sad, sad that he was about to pass through the valley of the shadow of death.

It was a bitter thing to watch him die. It was sweet to know he knew the Lord. It really was a bittersweet story...

Epilogue

To clear my mind and rest my soul and nurture my heart, I love to rake or mow or plow or putter around out on Bittersweet Farm. Standing out under the trees when Canada geese or Sandhill cranes call overhead is good for your soul. The scent of wood smoke, the blue October sky, the shocking beauty of morning when snow and frost white-out the landscape as far as you can see are stimulating in ways even wordy people cannot adequately describe.

When I'm mowing or raking or plowing or tinkering or puttering, I'm always thinking, and usually I'm thinking about the goodness of God. I'm remembering his direction, his protection, his provision through the years.

When I was young, I used to read the stories of well-known Christian leaders, pastors, missionaries, and the founders of great ministries. Their stories were remarkable. Of course they had remarkable stories. They were remarkable people. The things that God allowed them to accomplish were faith-building. Their lives make good reading.

After forty years of pastoral ministry and faithfully recording the things that God has done, the needs he has met, the direction he has given, I realize that the stories that God has written in my own life are as faith-building as anything else I have ever read anywhere. I was wrong. God does not write remarkable stories into the lives of men and women so much because they are worthy. He does that because that is just who he is. It's not so much because they are good as it is because he is good.

Not all hardships will be resolved before Jesus comes back. Not all wrongs will be made right in this world. Not all injustice will be judged in our lifetime, but I do hope the story of finding Bittersweet will stir your heart, stimulate your faith, and warm your soul, so that you will always trust and never doubt the promises of God. Even in a broken world full of injustice and abuse, you can build your life on the promises of God.

So now you have read some of our stories. They are stories I needed to tell, stories I never want to forget, because it is every bit as wonderful and faith-building as any story I have ever read. I hope they build your faith; you have stories to tell. I trust you will see the good hand of God, even in the bad things that come into your life. That you will always taste the sweet among the bitter.

Mark Haavisto was the chairman of the Bethel pulpit committee. In January of 2018, Mark came with the men from Bethel to move us. When we left, James Cumings and his dad, Pastor Leo drove the moving van. Mark drove Grenfell, my white Toyota. Lois drove her car. I drove out to Bittersweet Farm in my red Jeep, and my heart was filled with joy every mile of the way. The Red Jeep Journey ended out on Bittersweet Farm.

Bittersweet Farm
February 2019

ACKNOWLEDGMENTS:

Many thanks to my brother Kevin. Few would ever read the thousands upon thousands of words that I have written without the eager encouragement and practical help of my organized, devoted little brother.

I would like to acknowledge the help of Donna Rees for her excellent work in editing this book. Thank you Lois Pierpont for the cover design. Thank you, David Parsons for your valuable friendship and intelligent insights.

Lois and I and our family will always remember with tender love the twenty-two families who supported us with financial gifts during the season of The Red Jeep Journeys. May God reward you for your kindness to our family.

Thanks to Bethel Church. I love you. I hope to get to love you well for a long time. You were there for us and we want to be there for you.

———————

— You can read more of Ken's writing:
www.kenpierpont.com

— You can find Ken on Instagram and Facebook

— You can write to Ken at ken@kenpierpont.com

— You can call Ken at 734-626-9810